A PICTUREBOOK ON THE WALL:
MEMOIR

Also by Elaine Margolis

PULSE
A NOVEL

A PICTUREBOOK ON THE WALL: MEMOIR

ELAINE MARGOLIS

Langdon Street Press
212 3rd Avenue North, Suite 570
Minneapolis, MN 55401
612-455-2293
www.langdonstreetpress.com

ISBN - 1-934938-10-6
ISBN - 978-1-934938-10-2
LCCN - 2008925929

Book sales for North America and international:
Itasca Books, 3501 Highway 100 South, Suite220
Minneapolis, MN 55416
Phone: 952.345.4488 (toll free 1.800.901.3480)
Fax: 952.920.0541; email to orders@itascabooks.com

Cover Design by Wes Moore
Typeset by James Arneson

Printed in the United States of America

To Marty

ILLUSTRATIONS

TABLE OF CONTENTS

PREFACE

Covering the length of a wall in my hallway is a parade of photographs, portraits, and other pictures of the members of my family, from ancestors long dead, to grandchildren growing up.

I find myself walking down this hallway often, examining the faces long gone, remembering them and all they contributed to my upbringing and understanding. At the top, along ancestor row, are old sepia prints from Russia, one showing my mother's family, the Perlmans, Aunt Bernice not yet born, my grandmother and grandfather sitting straight, my mother, Jeannette, her long hair pulled back with a giant bow, young Uncle George standing behind her, baby Uncle Sammy between his mother and father. In another portrait, of my father's family, the Allens, my father, Samuel Allen, stands behind his seated father who is wearing a bowler hat, his mother holding younger brother Uncle Hy, older brother Uncle Ben seated in her lap. Next in line, an old photo of Grandma Bessie, my father's mother. Then, a portrait of Aunt Sara, my father's only sister, young and smiling as she was then. Aunt Sara is alive today, in her late 90's, still vibrant and in touch.

Below them on the wall are Uncle George and his violin, another portrait of my mother and Uncle George as children, my mother a little girl about six years old with long hair flowing down her back, wearing an old-fashioned white dress. Uncle George in Russian clothes, holding her hand, not more than eight, standing as straight as he always stood, even after he reached the age of one hundred.

A photo of the three siblings, my mother, Aunt Bernice and Uncle George, when they were much older. Uncle Sammy, their younger brother, was long dead by then. I think the only portrait of Sammy in existence sits beside his brother and sisters, a small thin likeness, the same Sammy with his mustache and crooked grin. A golden portrait of Aunt Bernice after she won a beauty contest hangs above a photo of her husband Saul, with his smart-alecky grin.

I lived in the same Chicago apartment with my family and my mother's family when I was small and circumstances forced us together. My mother's mother is not on the wall except in the antique portrait from Russia. Somehow she never sat still long enough to be captured.

Her husband, the grandfather I never knew, sits nearby in his wagon, his horse tethered in front, ready to start on his rounds, selling toys, tobacco and anything else he could peddle. A tall, handsome man, with an obvious resemblance to his oldest son George, he sits erect in his wagon, dark hair tousled, the picture of confidence and good will.

Next to him, a portrait of my father when he was about seven, seated on a chair, legs crossed at the ankles, chin on one hand, his serious expression foretelling his future gravitas.

My brother Marty is there, looking handsome in his Army uniform. Poor Marty. Life dealt him a series of unsurvivable blows, one of which was having a sister like me.

I'm on the wall too, a baby with a pudgy hand on a goldfish bowl, not quite ready to grab the fish inside. In another portrait I'm a child of about five, my straight hair framing a face with an uncharacteristically angelic expression. I have another photo, in a book somewhere, of me, gawky at eight, hair fastened with a hairbow almost as big as my head, its jaunty angles resembling wings about to carry me away. And, maybe, eventually, they did.

Many other photos and portraits hang on the wall, of family members still living. But the faces from the past are gone, except for their presence on my wall and in my memory.

Uncle George and my mother Jeannette

CHAPTER 1

THE DEPRESSION

I n 1929, when the stock market crashed, my mother's family, the Perlmans, moved into our apartment with us. According to the conversation I overheard in the kitchen, (I was four years old and listened to everything) my father had invested my grand-mother's money and the savings of my aunt and two uncles in the stock market and he had lost it all.

My mother, standing at the stove cooking my father's eggs, turned to face him.

"What did you say?"

"Well, you know, everyone said buying on margin was safe and we'd all make money. I thought it was a good investment."

My father, dressed for work in his tie and suit coat, stared miserably at my mother. He looked so sad I wanted to run over and hug him but my mother, hands on her hips, was getting ready to tell him a thing or two. She never yelled. She didn't have to yell. One look, that was all.

She turned back to the stove and emptied the eggs onto a plate that she placed in front of him, her expression severe. A frown wrinkled her forehead. Watching from the other side of the table where I was eating my cereal, her expression frightened me and tears started falling into my breakfast. Nobody noticed.

"Well, in that case," my mother said, "I guess they'll have to live with us. You, at least have a good salary. (My father worked as a lawyer at City Hall downtown.) We'll be all right. But my mother, it was all the money she had. And my brothers and sister, they're just starting out."

Before he could answer, she added, "That's the only solution," giving my father a look that made him bend over with guilt.

Kitchen sounds, including me sobbing into my cereal, echoed from the stove with its clanking and fearsome smell of gas whenever someone turned it on, to the kitchen sink, dripping and groaning when the tap was opened. In the nearby pantry the icebox sang its usual ka-chink, ka-chink. All familiar sounds but to me that morning they were scary.

After breakfast I took refuge in my favorite hiding place, behind the grand piano in the living room, where I kept my picture books. I thought about what I had just seen and heard, my mother angry, my father sad, markets crashing, had anyone been hurt? People moving in. That was the best part. I felt better thinking about the people moving in.

I loved it when everyone arrived – Uncle George with his violin, Uncle Sammy with his quiet smile under the thin moustache he sported, and beautiful Aunt Bernice, always kind and sweet to me. It was crowded in our two-bedroom, one bathroom apartment, but I didn't care. There was so much going on that my parents, for the most part, forgot to check on what I was doing. My aunt and uncles would pat me on the head, pick me up to kiss me, and some-times give me candy when my mother wasn't looking.

"Elaine? Look what I brought you." Aunt Bernice would slip me a small doll or a forbidden candy bar.

Dinnertime was noisy, everyone gathered around the dining room table, my mother and grandmother and aunt bringing in the food, my grandmother, red in the face from exertion, talking all the while as she went back and forth, "Here, put the meat next to the potatoes, no, move the salad there," and on and on. My mother complained, "I don't know if I can eat this. My stomach hurts. Maybe I'll make some eggs."

My aunt carried in the platters silently. I could tell she was upset at having to help after working hard all day. Even more upset at having to move in with us and give up her apartment. "Because," as she said, "I couldn't afford to keep it on just my salary."

Everyone talked a lot about the Depression, how friends were out of work, and families were helping each other all over Chicago, all over the country.

Uncle George gave violin lessons to make extra money but there were few people who could afford them. Mostly, he traveled around the country with his string quartet, giving concerts.

"Bookings are slow. People aren't interested in music when they haven't enough to eat." His head was bent over his plate, forehead creased with worry. Uncle George was tall with brown hair and a quick smile. People thought he was handsome. I thought he was wonderful, tall and straight and elegant, and he made the most beautiful music with his violin.

Aunt Bernice chimed in. "So far my job is safe but who knows for how long?" She was the beauty of the family with blonde hair and big blue eyes.

My grandmother finally sat down. "Do you ever think about getting married? What about that boy you've been going with? You should think about it. A husband would support you."

My grandmother was small with a gray bun of hair at the back of her head. She always wanted everyone to eat, especially me, and told them what she thought they should do. She talked constantly, a new undercurrent of sound in the apartment.

"Oh, Ma! It's a bad time to do that. People can't support them-selves, much less someone else." Aunt Bernice liked to keep to herself. She didn't like anyone telling her what to do, especially when she was tired and hungry and not liking the dinner any better than the rest of us.

I was sitting next to my mother who was cutting up the meat I had already decided not to eat. She picked up my fork, put a bite of meat and some potato on it, she knew I liked potatoes, and held it to my mouth.

"Elaine, don't be stubborn. You have to eat something."

I turned my head away. "I don't like that. It's hard to chew." My mother started to insist, but my father broke in.

"Let her alone, hon. The meat is a little tough. She can eat vegetables and salad."

My mother started to object and then she saw my other uncle, Sammy, nodding his head and grinning in agreement as he diligently chewed a mouthful. She put down the fork and frowned.

I was more interested in what everyone was saying than in the food, which was usually tough, flavorless and looked as bad as it tasted. My mother, claiming an ulcer, made sure that everything was overcooked and underseasoned, and then ate something else. She and my grandmother had a constant tug of war over the cooking.

By that time I could read a little. My mother bought books with large pictures and large printed words that she pointed to as she read so I was able to follow her finger and hear the sounds of the words.

Because my mother and grandmother were so busy with their ongoing argument about who was going to cook and who was going to clean up ("Ma! It's my kitchen," my mother wailed. "What! I should sit on my hands all day?" my grandmother shot back) I was left alone with things I would never have been allowed to go near, such as the books in my parents' bookcase where I tried to figure out the words. I slipped into the living room, hiding behind the grand piano next to the bookcases, and sat on the floor, a book open in my lap, my finger moving over the page.

I couldn't really tell what the books said but I knew the sounds and I liked the rhythm of the sentences as they flowed past my pointing finger. I spent every minute I could behind the piano.

4

When I wasn't trying to decipher the books, I made up stories, playing with my paper dolls. I would transport the dolls to faraway places, places I had never seen, places in my imagination, peopled with wondrous beasts and fabulous beings, sometimes acting out stories my mother had read to me. But mostly making everything up.

Behind the piano, which occupied most of the living room, I lived an imaginary life, peopled with children my age, children who did not exist in my real life. At the age of four or five, it didn't seem to matter much. In the dim light coming from the windows on either side of a permanently unlit fireplace, the contents of the bookshelves under the windows offered a ready source of enchantment, even though I couldn't make out what they said, not yet. And my imaginary friends liked everything I liked and did everything I did. I was safe and happy behind the piano, secure in my imaginary world.

The sleeping arrangements in our apartment were tight. I was about five years old then, still in the crib in my parents' bedroom. My grandmother took the second bedroom with my Aunt Bernice.

My aunt worked as a secretary to a lawyer downtown. She was always coming home from work and exclaiming as she walked in the door, "I can't stand working for that man one more minute!" But she would always go back to work the next day as if nothing had happened. I thought this was very puzzling.

Aunt Bernice's blonde hair puffed about her face, her blue eyes sparkled, and she was slim and shapely. Everybody in the family admired her looks and sweet nature. She went out with different men and I heard my mother say she would get married soon and move out and then I could sleep in the room with my grandmother and get out of my crib. I didn't know whether I liked that or not.

Uncle George made the sleeping porch his bedroom. He liked the privacy at the back of the apartment, where he could practice his violin for hours. When he wasn't on tour with his string quartet, he practiced almost non-stop and sometimes he let me sit in the room and listen if I was very quiet. He made wonderful sounds with his violin; it made me think of the music the sentences made in my secret reading place behind the piano. He called his music sonatas, concertos, names I liked but whose meanings I couldn't figure out.

Since the sleeping porch was surrounded on three sides by drafty windows it was cold in there in the winter with the door shut. When my mother found me (she could never find me behind the piano) she made me leave so I wouldn't catch cold. She burst in, interrupting Uncle George, who frowned and stopped playing.

"It's freezing in here, Elaine. Look, your nose is running. You have to come with me." My mother wiped my nose with the tissue she always carried and pulled me out the door.

"She's not bothering me, you know," Uncle George muttered. "She can stay, you know, with a sweater."

"No, No. She can do something else. Where it's warm." She closed the door firmly and said, "Elaine, you don't want to get sick, do you?"

I shook my head. I was so angry I couldn't say anything. She was always afraid I would get sick, mostly when I was having fun. I did get sick a lot, only because my immune system never had a chance to build up since I was rarely close to anyone who had any germs. Germs, my mother's nemesis. She interrupted my times with my uncles and aunt, shouted for me when I was hiding behind the piano, upset my imaginary life. Otherwise she didn't pay attention to me, except when she was reading to me.

She hurried off to answer the telephone. I stayed where I was, listening outside the door.

Chicago in winter was so cold the windows were covered with frost in beautiful patterns. I liked to trace them with my finger as I listened to my uncle play in the sleeping porch when my mother wasn't home. He asked me if I would like to learn the violin. I said I wanted to learn to play the piano in the living room the way Aunt Bernice did. She made the whole house rumble and thunder when she pounded the keys. Her favorite piece (and mine too) was Enesco's "Roumanian Rhapsody No. 2." I would love to make the kind of giant noise she made when she played the piano.

To my mind what my uncle played was music, what my aunt played was beautiful noise. There was always music playing somewhere in the house, especially on Sundays when Uncle George had the symphony on. It would put me to sleep, soft and hypnotic. As I grew older it made me impatient. I wanted to hear songs from the Hit Parade and other popular tunes. My family turned up their collective noses at the thought.

Uncle George and his violin.

CHAPTER 2

UNCLES

My grandmother bemoaned the fact that Uncle George had gone to medical school and quit before he finished because he didn't have enough time for his music. Then he went to law school, passed the bar and decided to go on the road on concert tours with the quartet he formed, and gave up the law too. My grandmother was sure he would starve. When he tired of traveling and sleeping in different hotels, he became a violin teacher downtown at the Fine Arts Building, started making money, and moved out. He supported my grandmother while she lived, and kept contributing to the rent on our apartment.

Uncle George, everyone else knew him as George Perlman, left a legacy of music, composing and publishing beautiful pieces for the violin. Over the years he became acquainted with many famous violinists, such as Yehudi Menuhin and Mischa Elman. Even Jack Benny was a friend of his.

He always had an anecdote to tell at family dinners. My favorite was the story about a student who was playing one of his compositions at her home in Los Angeles and looked out the window to see a little white-haired man -- his hair wild about his head -- standing outside her window as she played. She went out to see what he wanted and he said he also played the violin and asked her what music she was playing. She told him and gave him my uncle's address. And that was how Uncle George befriended Albert Einstein.

Uncle George was the kind of man who was always inquiring into other worlds, other disciplines. Music and the violin remained his first priority but I remember when he became intrigued with spiritualism. The occult captured him and he began going to séances. At one of them he met Sir Arthur Conan Doyle, better known as the author of the Sherlock Holmes books, but also an authority on the spirit world.

At one dinner Uncle George regaled us with an account of a disembodied trumpet that played at the request of someone's dead relative. The trumpet traveled around the séance unassist- ed, tootling away. He was amazed by this and insulted when the family nodded politely and snickered behind their napkins. He was always trying to carry us along on his latest enthusiasm.

I, having heard of Sherlock Holmes by then (I was almost eight and reading everything I could find), was more interested in the author aspect of Conan Doyle than the ghost factor, although I must admit, I was a little intrigued. Like Uncle George, I believed everything was possible until it was proven wrong or mistaken.

Then he persuaded my parents to go with him to a séance so my mother could talk to their long-dead father. I begged and pleaded to go along but my parents refused to take me.

I couldn't wait to hear a report from my mother the next day. She debunked the whole event, said it was a big fake. She could see the people behind the door running the séance and thought it was terrible that they were taking advantage of the gullibility of strangers.

I was very disappointed and the next time I saw Uncle George, when he came over to visit my grandmother, I asked him. He smiled and said, "It was quite interesting, you know. I'm sorry your parents wouldn't let you come along. You would have enjoyed meeting Sir Conan Doyle. He's a fascinating man, but now he's gone back to England, having completed his studies of the occult in this country."

I asked again about the séance, whether he had spoken with my grandfather.

"Unfortunately the circumstances weren't quite right for our little experiment. The medium was not feeling well and her powers were weak. I felt badly that I had dragged your mother and father out to see a failed event. But maybe we can arrange it again." My mother refused the offer.

At another dinner he told us about his meeting and subsequent friendship with Harry Houdini, the famous magician and escape artist. Uncle George was endlessly fascinated by people who he felt were stretching the envelope of the world we knew and the world we didn't know.

By the time Uncle George met Houdini, he had decided that the practitioners of the occult were charlatans and their claims of reaching dead loved ones were fake, all fake. Houdini was one of their chief critics, another reason Uncle George and he became friends. Houdini said the ruses they used to fool people were nothing more than magic tricks, not even good magic tricks.

None of this made Uncle George think any less of the possibility of a spirit world, another dimension, a place we could not reach while alive. And since no one could prove or disprove it, I agreed with him that we should keep our options open. But then, I usually agreed with him.

Uncle George was sure he knew the real reason Houdini had died and it wasn't because of a failed escape, as many thought. He was sure none of Houdini's tricks had done him in. He never said what he thought had killed him, though Houdini had hinted that he was ill, suffering from mysterious stomach pains. Much later I found out that Houdini had died of peritonitis from a burst appendix. Not glamorous or mysterious, but at least he was human.

After Uncle George had moved out of our apartment - to my great regret - my father finally was able to listen to the Cubs baseball broadcasts on Sunday. My father would never put his wishes before anyone else's in the house.

Uncle George knew nothing about the Cubs. Music was his world and he loved living in it. He taught the violin until a month before he died, at the age of 103 in the year 2000, his life touching three centuries, hard for me to imagine.

My younger uncle, Sammy, was a dentist, so my grandmother didn't worry about him. She had too much to do worrying about everyone else. As it turned out, he was the one she should have worried about most. First, he had tuberculosis and then, later, cancer.

Uncle Sammy left his own legacy, crocheting colorful wool afghans for everyone in the family, to keep his fingers limber, he said. My healthy teeth came, I'm sure, from the special care he gave me when I was small. He was so gentle and soft-spoken, his voice never rose above a whisper.

He would tell me stories about the people who came to get their teeth fixed, how he was able to take care of them so they weren't hurt or uncomfortable. He talked about their children and their lives, ordinary lives, but I was always interested, his voice was so soft, his manner so gentle. And I knew he spoke the truth about not hurting anyone, since he had never hurt me, even when he was drilling a deep cavity. I had very few of those.

He married but then had to go to a tuberculosis sanatorium and shortly afterward his wife divorced him. He didn't know he had cancer. After they declared him free of TB, he moved in with us again and went back to his dental practice. His patients returned because he was so good at his work and didn't charge much. But his stomach kept hurting and he kept ignoring the pain and dosing himself with strong painkillers. Then it was too late and he faded quietly from our lives.

I was not allowed to go to his funeral. I was never allowed to go to any funeral of anyone I knew who died. To save me from the grief, my mother said. As if it did.

While Uncle Sammy lived with us, he slept on a cot in the dining room. Aunt Bernice had moved into the sleeping porch after Uncle George left, and I eventually joined her there, some years later.

Uncle Sammy

CHAPTER 3

THE APARTMENT

A word about the apartment we lived in -- I called it That Place. It was on the Northwest Side of Chicago, a street lined with bungalows, one-story homes typical of the city. We lived in the only apartment building on the block, three stories high. Since we were on the second floor, anyone who wanted to come up had to ring a bell in the lobby.

The apartment stretched narrowly from a front hall where the telephone sat on its tiny table, the first thing you saw when you came in the door, located so anyone in the apartment could hear any phone conversation going on. It was my grandmother's favorite spot, listening to everyone's phone calls, especially mine.

To the left of the hall was the master bedroom, my crib in one corner, near the window. It was the sunniest room in the house, its one window sending more light into the house than any other room.

Off the front hallway was the living room and beyond that the front sun room, surrounded on three sides by windows like the sleeping porch in the back. This is where we all sat around listening to the radio, on couches under the windows, after dinner every night, when my parents weren't going out.

Down a hallway was the only bathroom, then past that, the kitchen on one side of the hall, a large dining room on the other and beyond it, the sleeping porch. Outside the kitchen was a porch, and stairs running down the back of the house.

There was a large yard with grass and not much else growing in it and beyond the yard an alley stretched past all the back yards on the block. Peddlers would make their way through this alley daily and I was forbidden to go near it, which made me want to go out there even more.

My grandmother said, "Peddlers are Gypsies. They kidnap little girls if they catch them in the alley. You don't want them to take you away, do you ?"

"What's a Gypsy?"

"Never mind," she said. "You don't need to know." This was her standard answer to most of my questions.

I was scared but I went in the alley anyway, looking cautiously up and down to see if anyone was coming. When I heard the peddlers shouting, calling out the things they sold, I ran up the stairs and into the house as fast as I could go.

Many years later I learned that my grandfather had been a peddler. I wondered at my grandmother's remark about Gypsies. But I didn't ask. I knew I wouldn't get an answer.

Next to our back yard was a small house where a family with two children lived. Sometimes I cut through the broken fence and visited them to play with the children, a boy and a girl near my age. My mother didn't like me to go there. She said, "The house is dirty, the people are too poor, the father is always out of work. I think it's not a good place for you."

I didn't care about any of that. The mother and father were very kind. They always welcomed me. "Elaine! We're so glad you came over. Let's have some milk and cookies. Here, I just baked them." And the mother set a plate with steaming cookies on the table with a pitcher of milk.

I played games with the children, like Tag or Hide and Seek or Jump Rope if I brought my rope. They had few toys, mostly broken. Sometimes I would hide a toy or two under my sweater and bring it over for them.

The things I did notice: the parents were missing some teeth, the family wore clothes that seemed about to tear, the fabric worn, some places already sewn together. There was a musty smell in the house, like dust so ingrained it could never be wiped away. Looking back. it seemed as though a pervading sadness hung over them. I tried my best to cheer them up. It was the one place I always wore a happy smile.

No one ever yelled at us, we were allowed to do what we wanted. Our only restriction was, "Don't go in the street."

When I heard my mother calling, I would leave, giving everyone a hug. I'd cut around to the front of our apartment building so my mother wouldn't know I had been doing something I was forbidden to do.

The warmth in that house, despite the sadness, nourished me. I played with those children secretly until the family had to move away because the landlord was going to tear down the house. Their leaving left a void in my life that took a long time to fill.

To me, years later, when I thought of them, they personified all the sadness and upheaval the Depression had caused.

In our apartment the sleeping porch had a twin bed on either side, and a dresser and small desk along a wall lined with windows. Eventually this became my room and I would spend long hours at that desk writing stories, living other lives I made up that I found more desirable.

A large table surrounded by many chairs took up most of the dining room. There was a heavy sideboard, loaded with the Good Dishes, which were only used when my parents had a dinner party.

The table and chairs in the kitchen where we ate breakfast and lunch, usually separately, were on one wall, opposite the frightening stove. I was warned repeatedly by my grandmother not to touch it, I could get burned, and so it became another hostile object, along with the sink in the corner, which made terrible noises when the water was running. Plumbing was not one of the finer features of That Place.

There were always dishes piled in the drainer on the sink, and garbage usually waited under the sink in a large can to be thrown out. My mother and grandmother were very particular about the garbage, always opening the kitchen door to throw the garbage into the big can on the back porch, letting in huge drafts, usually while I was eating.

Near the back door was a walk-in pantry where the canned goods, the dishes and other household things were kept. When my grandmother made cookies and cakes, and her specialty, strudel, she would hide them on top of the refrigerator, really it was an ice-box for much of my childhood, with the iceman delivering huge chunks of dripping ice every morning.

I would try my best to reach the goodies and sometimes I succeeded, on top of a stepladder kept nearby. Once I ate half a recipe of strudel. I hid behind the piano, my face full of tell-tale crumbs, my mother shouting, "Elaine? Elaine? Where are you? Come here this minute," my grandmother muttering in the background, "You ate the strudel. It took me all day to make it. Now there's not enough and I worked all day."

But I couldn't resist. The flaky sweet crust filled with raisins and prunes was so delectable, my mouth watered at the thought of eating one piece. Once I started, I couldn't stop. The pieces went down so easily, I stuffed them in my mouth, one after the other. I knew I would get in trouble but the delicious haze I was in was worth it.

The uproar my mother and grandmother made over the strudel was terrible. My mother yelled, my grandmother sobbed. You'd think they would have been happy I was eating something. Usually I consumed very little and was skinny and always sick. Cowering behind the piano, I didn't feel sick at all. I felt wonderful.

My punishment was no dessert for dinner. I didn't care. I didn't even eat dinner.

In the living room the grand piano, my secret hiding place, dominated the narrow room. Later, when I was much older, the collection of books on the shelves, books I had tried and finally succeeded in reading, filled me with disdain, only a few of the books, I felt, worthy of further notice. When I left home I took two books -- "Anthony Adverse" and "An Introduction to Psychoanalysis" by Sigmund Freud. Any book held the promise of magic but those two had to come with me wherever I went. I still have them.

Beyond the living room was the sun room with the couches and the radio, the gathering place after dinner (we didn't talk, we listened), the place I spent my time in the evening when everyone had gone out and I was alone with my grandmother who went to her room early. I listened to the programs, the comedians, the dramas, the Hit parade, anything I could find to amuse me. In 1938 I heard Orson Welles frighten everyone with his famous broadcast about Martians invading Earth, and was surprised to find out people actually believed it.

Grandfather Perlman and his horse

CHAPTER 4

CHICKEN POX

One evening, some years before, when we were sitting around the radio in the sunroom, my mother announced to my grandmother and me, I was six at the time, that she was pregnant. My father, beaming, his arm around her, was so happy, his whole personality changed after the announcement.

Usually quiet and vague, daydreaming and not hearing what people said to him, he became lively and smiled all the time. He laughed at everything and hugged me, even though my mother told him not to get too near me, I might catch something. She never stopped worrying about my catching something.

Where would they put the new baby? Why, in the crib, of course. I didn't know it at the time but I resented the fact that I was being evicted from my parents' room by some upstart baby that probably wouldn't even be a sister.

My mother grew bigger and bigger and crankier and crankier. She hobbled around and sighed a lot and clutched her stomach. The whole house waited on her and did whatever she wanted. I just stayed out of her way.

While she was in the hospital having the baby, I caught the chicken pox. Really bad. Everything I caught was really bad since I had never been able to build up resistance to anything. (My grandmother had told me once that when I was a baby in a carriage, my mother would wheel me down the street dressed in a white nurse's uniform with a mask on her face.)

Tossing in the rumpled crib with a high fever, I missed my mother. She had a lot of faults but she sure knew how to take care of me when I was sick. I decided it was because she had so much practice.

I was almost too big for the crib, tall for my six years, thrashing around and yelling, "I itch!" "I itch!" and my grandmother had to stop cooking -- she had won the battle of the kitchen, since my mother was in the hospital and not able upstage her -- and she would run into the bedroom and smear me with calamine lotion. It helped for about five minutes.

"If you scratch the itches," she warned me, "you'll get terrible marks on your face and body that will never go away."

She frightened me so thoroughly I held on to the bars of the crib to keep from scratching myself, except for a place on the side of my nose where, sure enough, I had a small mark when the pox were gone. She dosed me with baby aspirin that didn't help much and wrapped me in cold sheets to take the fever down. All it did was make me itch more.

Since I was contagious for a long time -- the pox formed scabs that were falling like snow everywhere -- my mother couldn't bring the baby home when she was let out of the hospital so she went to my Aunt Sophie Allen's house for a couple of weeks while I recuperated. My Aunt Sophie, married to my father's younger brother, Howard, who we all called Hy, was my mother's closest friend in my father's family. She was full of fun and warm and generous. No one but Aunt Sophie would have volunteered to take in my mother and her baby.

I was so angry that my mother had had a boy and wasn't coming home to take care of me, I didn't talk to her at all when she finally brought home the little screaming creature who had kicked me out of my bed. Not that she noticed.

My mother, father and grandmother made a terrible fuss about cleaning out my parents' bedroom and sterilizing the crib.

"Don't come in here, Elaine. Can't you see we're trying to get things ready for the baby?"

They made me feel like I was unclean and a nuisance. But then I felt that way anyhow after the chicken pox. I wasn't allowed to go near the baby for weeks. My mother and her germ thing.

I hated it when I saw myself in the mirror because I looked so awful, thin and gangly with straight short hair and a big nose, scabs stuck to my face. I secretly wished I had not grown older than the cute little girl of two and a half in the photo I had of us on vacation in the North Woods. The North Woods, a place in time I wanted back.

The Perlmans, my mother Jeannette lower left

CHAPTER 5

THE NORTH WOODS

It was so long ago it comes back to me in a haze, a haze of misty sunlight shining through tall leafy trees on a lake so blue it looked painted. But I remember Uncle Jack, my mother's uncle, a jolly outgoing man whose life's passion was fishing.

We visited Uncle Jack the summer I was two. The month of August was his time to go fishing in the North Woods. He left his family of two small boys and my Aunt Jeannette home every year, insisting he needed time to think and be alone. But he had invited my mother, my father and me for two glorious weeks.

Uncle Jack was always smiling his big smile. He picked me up and swung me around and roared with delight when we arrived.

"Hello, cutie!" he shouted as we got out of the car. Back then, I was very cute, with a Dutch boy haircut, my straight black hair a cap around my chubby face and big black eyes that never stopped looking things over.

Uncle Jack was dressed in a red and black flannel shirt and baggy pants, his hands red from being in water, from pulling out fish and fishhooks, he told me. My father was dressed his usual way: starched white shirt, tie perfectly tied under his collar and a dark suit. My mother was in heels and pearls. I had on a little white dress and Mary Janes. But that all changed the next morning.

I woke up early, listening to birds singing so loudly I thought at first they were in the cabin with us. It was very cold. I would have to wear a sweater if it didn't warm up. My mother would make sure of that.

I ran outside to see what the weather was like. I knew my mother would be angry with me outside in my pajamas. My way of getting even for her constantly telling me what I couldn't do. After all, I was two and a half, old enough to make my way from one room to the other. I was very sure about what I wanted and what I didn't want. My mother and I had constant differences of opinion about this, which I usually lost.

The cabin was built of logs with a window in one corner, a small bed for me. I had never slept in a real bed before, being confined to a crib at home. I liked it without the bars. I felt free. But then the North Woods was a time of freedom for me. At the time, I didn't know what that meant. I just knew I liked it.

My parents slept in a larger bed behind a curtain, only drawn at night. One wall of the cabin was the kitchen with a wood burning stove and an old icebox that took real ice. There was a table in the middle of the room with four chairs, the only places to sit unless we sat on the beds.

Outside I found my father dressed like Uncle Jack. I had never seen him without a tie. At first I didn't know who he was, a stranger in a plaid flannel shirt. His back was to me and he stood awkwardly in front of a tree stump with a piece of wood poised on top. He was holding a large axe and was raising it over his head. Just then, my mother ran around the corner of the cabin, dressed in one of her housedresses, and black tied shoes.

She yelled, "Stop! You're going to cut yourself!"

He started and dropped the axe, barely missing his foot.

"My God! You scared me. Don't ever do that again!" In one motion he picked up the axe and gave the wood a giant whack. It fell neatly into two pieces.

I yelled, "Hooray!" and they both turned and saw me.

"Elaine, come into the cabin at once!" my mother said in a tight voice, her lips barely moving. "You'll catch a cold out here with nothing on."

By then the sun had broken through the overhanging tree branches and was warming the air, me, and everything around me. I looked up as far as I could stretch my neck and saw the treetops miles above.

I wanted to stay outside but my mother grabbed my arm and hustled me into the house. "I have to dress you and brush your teeth. Daddy will cut the wood and light the fire in the stove and then I'll make us a nice breakfast."

"Where's Uncle Jack?"

"He's getting everything ready to take you and Daddy fishing. Won't you like that?"

I liked anything I could do with Uncle Jack. I hardly ever saw him in Chicago. He and his family lived on the far South Side – we lived Northwest, a continent away, it seemed. I smiled, erasing my habitual frown. Since not much pleased me in those early days, the frown had grown on my face like a wart.

My mother pulled out a cotton shirt for me and some overalls and gym shoes. I had never seen those clothes before. In summer I was usually dressed in dresses and little sandals. I loved the idea of wearing the new clothes. Maybe she would let me run through the woods in them. Maybe even climb a tree. I didn't object, as I always did, to her dressing me. She wouldn't ever let me dress myself. Luckily I watched her closely to learn how to do it.

Just then my father carried in the wood. He pushed it in the stove with some paper and lit a match and closed the stove door. He had a cut on one hand and his shirt was torn.

"What did you do to yourself?" My mother rushed over. "Let me fix that cut before you get an infection. You know how easily you get infections."

She rolled up his sleeve and poured water from a big bucket over the cut. There was a sink but it didn't have running water. We had to get the water from the lake, which my mother boiled. She had complained all the way to the North Woods that this was going to be very hard, very unsanitary. When she saw the outhouse behind our cabin I thought she would get right into the car and make my father drive us back. She had brought a portable toilet seat for me that she placed over the hole in the outhouse. She sprayed the outhouse with Lysol after every use.

"Ouch!" my father said as she poured iodine on the cut. She always used iodine. When I scraped my knees and I saw her coming with that brown bottle I ran and hid and didn't come out until I saw the red mercurochrome bottle in her hand. Those were the only remedies she knew. Maybe they were the only ones available at the time. It was 1928.

The stove had started to smoke and my mother scrambled some eggs and put coffee up. Soon we sat down to our first meal in the North Woods. I was used to having cereal but my mother said I needed something hot because the mornings were so cold. It was hard to believe it was August and back home in Chicago we had been in a heat wave.

The eggs and hot bread and milk tasted good and I ate a lot. My mother was very pleased. Then there was a large knock on the door and Uncle Jack was in the doorway with fishing poles in one hand and a big bucket in the other.

"Hello gorgeous!" he said to me. "Are you ready to go fishing?"

"Oh, yes!" I had no idea what that meant but if Uncle Jack wanted to do it I was ready. And then when I found out my mother wasn't going -- "I'll just stay here and tidy up. Do the dishes, wash out some clothes" -- I was really happy. At last I was going somewhere without her watching my every move. My father came along with us, looking a little apprehensive about whether he could manage the fishing. I knew he could do it, even though he was a little vague about things sometimes. My mother did the thinking for all of us, whether we wanted her to or not.

As we went out the door she was putting a huge pot of water on the stove.

"Bring back fish for supper," she called. "And be sure to keep an eye on Elaine. She can't swim."

In the boat, the wind blew hot. I pulled off my sweater. No one said anything. How wonderful! Uncle Jack had given me a small pole with a hook on the end. He reached into his bucket and took out a big worm.

"We're going to put this worm on the end of your hook," he said. "Then you put the pole in the water and wait for a fish to bite."

I settled onto the little bench that crossed the boat. Uncle Jack said it was a rowboat, and pointed to the two oars he had used to get us into the lake. The sun was warm and a breeze made wavy ruffles on the water. The lake, surrounded by huge trees covered to the ground with leaves and branches, reflected the green wall around it.

My father was sitting stiffly in the center of the boat, grasping a pole. He held on with both hands, while I let my pole hang loosely. I was wondering if I should grab it with my other hand when Uncle Jack gave a shout. He was on the bench next to me, to make sure I didn't fall overboard.

"I caught something," he shouted, holding onto his pole. The end was deep in the water. Suddenly a fish jumped out of the water on the end of his pole. I was so excited I almost dropped my pole.

"Look! Look!" I jumped up and down on the bench while Uncle Jack held onto his pole and turned the little wheel near the handle.

"See?" he said. "I'm working the fish so that I can bring it in." He pulled hard on the pole and the fish sailed into the air and landed on the floor of the boat, gasping and wriggling.

My father said, "Don't get near it, Elaine."

I was too excited to listen. I leaned over the fish to get a good look as Uncle Jack picked it up and took the hook out of its mouth. He threw it into a basket in the corner of the boat and put another worm on his hook. The fish eyed me with a grimace.

"He smiled at me!" I shouted.

"Who wouldn't smile at you," Uncle Jack said, patting my knee. "That's a pretty good sized fish. Your mother will be happy. Now let's see if we can get one for you."

He moved my pole up and back in the water and then I felt a pull on the end and almost lost it. I grabbed hard and yelled, "I got one!"

Uncle Jack helped me and we pulled in another fish, smaller than his, but he said it was big enough to keep. He took it off the hook and threw it in with the other fish which had stopped moving.

We rocked in the boat, our poles bobbing in the water and felt the breeze on our faces. I shook my pole, hoping to attract another fish.

As the morning passed, my father was more relaxed, smiling a lot and chatting with Uncle Jack.

"I understand you're thinking about going to law school," Uncle Jack said.

My father nodded. "Accounting is all right but I've decided what I really want to do is be a judge. Law school is the first step."

Uncle Jack's eyes widened. "Really! That's just swell!" He slapped my father on the back with his free hand. My father beamed.

I had never seen him look so happy with a little smile hovering around his eyes all morning. He even began to catch some fish. In fact he was doing better at it than Uncle Jack and even a lot better than I.

I jumped up and hugged him, something I would never do with my mother around, and he grabbed me.

"Be careful! You're rocking the boat." But he held me tightly and didn't let go for a while.

I really liked this fishing, even though I didn't think the fish were too happy about it. My two-year-old mind was always working. If they kept biting our worms off the hook and getting caught, I figured they didn't know any better, something my mother would always say about people.

When it was lunchtime, Uncle Jack paddled the boat over to a little island in the middle of the lake and we jumped out, my father carrying Uncle Jack's basket while he tied up the boat.

"This is the best part," Uncle Jack said. "A picnic in the woods."

While they were putting down a blanket and unpacking the lunch, I ran around the clearing on the shore of the lake and then ventured into the woods nearby.

It was very quiet and warm, with insects humming in my ears and birds singing in the treetops. I looked up and saw a large bird circling, his wings stretched out straight. Then he dove into the water going so fast I almost lost him, and came out with a fish in his beak. We weren't the only ones fishing, I thought.

I ran around, happy to explore and touch and smell everything with no one to stop me. Then I heard my father.

"Elaine! Lunch is ready."

I hadn't been hungry until then. In fact food was something I really didn't care about and the more my parents urged me to eat the less I wanted to. But now my stomach was rumbling, and I ran back to the blanket. I was sure lunch would be something good, since Uncle Jack had brought it.

He handed me a sandwich wrapped in paper. It was a bologna sandwich, he said. I had never seen it before. I sniffed. Smelled good. I licked it. Hmm. Then I took a bite. It was a little spicy, something I wasn't allowed to eat, so I gobbled it up, even though it seemed a little rubbery and I choked because I didn't chew it enough.

My father patted me on the back and said, "Jen doesn't give Elaine lunch meats. In fact she only feeds her things she makes herself. Did you like it, honey?"

"It's okay," I said, not wanting to be impolite but reaching for a large peach and a banana. There were cookies too. And pop. I had never tasted pop. I liked it a lot. It was sweet and tickled my nose.

"Let's clean this stuff up and get back to work," Uncle Jack said, shaking the crumbs off the blanket for the birds and bugs.

"We should be able to get in a couple more hours and bring back a big catch for dinner. You're coming to my cabin. I'll clean the fish and grill them over an open fire. You never tasted anything so good." He smacked his lips at me and I laughed. He was so funny. I liked everything he did.

As we climbed back in the boat, I yawned. I always had to take a nap after lunch, not that I wanted to, but my mother said it was good for me. I hardly ever slept, playing with the toys in my crib or just lying there, looking out the window and wishing I was grown up and didn't have to waste all this time.

My father said, "Are you tired? You can lie down in the boat on the blanket. We can fix a little bed for you and you can take your nap."

"No, thanks." I hopped in and reached for my pole. "We need to catch some more fish. I'll help."

Both men roared. In fact they laughed at everything I said, even if it wasn't funny. It felt so good that we were all having such a good time. My father especially. He didn't look like he was having fun when he was home.

"I think our little lady is becoming an experienced fisherman. Pretty soon we won't be able to get her out of the boat." Uncle Jack gave me a quick hug and went back to baiting our hooks. He smelled a little fishy but I didn't care. I probably did too.

Pretty soon my arms were tired from holding the pole and pulling it in to see if something was on the end. I curled up on top of my sweater in the bottom of the boat and snoozed. The water rocked me and the wind soothed me and I had a dream where I was riding on a big fish out into the water and having a wonderful time with all the fishes.

Uncle Jack woke me when he picked me up and carried me to our cabin. The sun had almost set and the air was cool again. I put my arms around his neck and gave him a big kiss.

"Well, thank you, lovie," he said. "I hope you had a good time today."

I nodded my head.

"Would you like to go again tomorrow?"

"Oh, yes. But could we have something else for lunch?"

He roared again. "You bet. I'll make us something wonderful. I'm going to the store to buy it right now."

My mother met us at the door. "Did you have fun?" Before I could answer she said, "Phew! You smell terrible! You need a bath." The next thing I knew she had ripped off my clothes and put me in the kitchen sink filled with sudsy water.

"Hey!" I said. The water was too hot, as usual, but I had to agree it felt good. As she scrubbed me she said, "I had a feeling you would be dirty when you came back so I made everything ready. Did you catch any fish?"

She was being nice so I told her about our day, leaving out the part about the bologna. I said we were going again tomorrow and Uncle Jack was making a really good lunch.

"Is that a fact?" she said. "Maybe I'll go too."

"You won't like the worms," I said, sorry I had been so enthusiastic. I could see our whole adventure sinking under the weight of her disapproving frown.

"I won't look," she said and pulled me out of the water where I was beginning to enjoy it. She rubbed me vigorously with the towel, a rough towel, not like the soft ones we had at home, and dressed me in my pajamas.

"Wait," I said. "We're going over to Uncle Jack's for a big fish dinner. I can't go in my pajamas."

"Oh, yes you can," she said. "You'll probably be asleep before we even finish."

And I was. The dinner tasted wonderful but my mother kept examining every mouthful before I ate it to make sure there were no bones. Finally I just gave up, put my head on the table and didn't know anything until the next morning when the birds woke me with their song.

The days in the North Woods ran into each other, one day in the boat the same as the days before. Uncle Jack brought cream cheese and jelly sandwiches after the bologna day. My father had told him they were my favorite. They tasted even better on the island, with the birds waiting for every crumb.

We were catching so much fish I was getting tired of eating it every night for dinner. No matter how my mother or Uncle Jack fixed it, it still tasted like fish and there was the nightly search for bones in every bite.

My mother noticed. She said to my father, "Elaine isn't going with you tomorrow. We'll walk into town and get something else for dinner. She could use a change of scenery."

My father said, "But Jen, she really likes fishing."

My mother shook her head and turned away.

I was very happy with the scenery. But I knew it was my mother who was getting tired of it. She hadn't really liked the fishing. She only went once and we had to go back right after lunch because she said I was getting sunburned and the bugs were biting me. Actually, she meant that about herself. I was always the cause of everything she needed to change. And now I was going to have to go into town to buy something to eat I would probably not touch, because she was getting bored with the scenery.

"Why do I have to go?" My frown came back. I knew I could get into trouble but I was still trying to save the next day. "Uncle Jack needs me to help with the fishing. He said so."

"I really don't want to go alone. Can't he get along without you for one day?"

Well, if she really wanted me to go—

"Okay," I said. "Will you buy me something in town?"

"Of course I will." So next day she put me into my white dress but let me wear my gym shoes because we were walking, and off we went.

The town was small with wooden buildings and a little store where my mother sniffed everything she picked up in the grocery department, finally settling on some chickens and vegetables. She knew I didn't like vegetables and would only eat chicken with lots of mashed potatoes. She didn't buy any potatoes.

"I'm not going to eat that," I said. I picked up a large can of spaghetti with both hands. "Let's have this."

"Now Elaine, Uncle Jack is coming for dinner and I know he loves chicken."

I knew she was only saying that to make me agree to the chicken but I didn't want to argue in the store. The ladies who waited on us and the other customers kept patting me on the head and saying how cute I was. I didn't want to spoil things by having a tantrum.

We bought dinner and then went across the street to the hardware store where they had a small toy department. My mother kept picking up dolls and games and books. "Do you like this?" "How about this?"

I wasn't going to take anything she picked out. I wanted to pick out my own toy. Finally I settled on a small figure of a woodsman in a red flannel shirt, carrying a toy axe.

"It looks like Daddy chopping wood," I said, liking the smiling face of the doll and his moving arms and legs. I moved the arm with the axe up and down.

"Oh, all right," my mother said with a disagreeable look, and paid for the doll. I could tell she didn't like it. It wasn't "little girl" enough for her.

We walked back in silence. I played with my doll, and my mother broke in every now and then with something I had to do when we went back to Chicago, like visit an elderly aunt, buy shoes, get a haircut, things I didn't want to think about up there in the North Woods with Uncle Jack and fishing, and where I could run free in the woods.

It seemed like a dream then, and as I look back, it seems like a dream now.

My mother Jeannette as a young woman

CHAPTER 6

SCHOOL

I didn't have any playmates when I was small. The boys and girls on my block were off-limits because my father was the precinct captain. My mother acted as if he was the king and I was the princess and couldn't play with the common subjects, as I did in my made-up stories.

I liked the children on my block and they liked me. Boys and girls of lower middle-class families, whose fathers worked in factories and other jobs my mother did not consider good enough or stylish enough.

One day when my mother was out having lunch with friends, I was playing baseball in the street with the neighborhood kids and I hit a home run. Everybody cheered as I raced around the bases.

"Yay Elaine!" "Run Elaine run!" When I hit home, they patted me on the back, slapped hands. "Good job." "You can really swing that bat!"

A couple of girls hugged me because our side won the game. Just then my mother came home and that was the end of that.

"Elaine! Come here this minute. What are you doing out there in the middle of the street?"

One minute of happiness a day was all I could expect, and sometimes not even that.

It sounds like my mother was mean and thoughtless, but I know now that she was trying so hard to bring me up right, what she thought was right, and she didn't have a clue as to how to do it. Her idea of "right" was what other people, her friends, thought. And my grandmother constantly prodded her to act this way and that.

"Tell Elaine she shouldn't play with those girls." "She spends too much time reading. She'll hurt her eyes." And on and on.

My father wasn't much help. When he was home he was off in a daze thinking about things we had no idea about, or reading the newspaper, or telling us stories at dinner about his law cases.

"There was a man who pretended to be hurt in a car crash and then when he was on the witness stand –" He elaborated on the story, his eyes shining, his voice animated.

I loved the stories, and especially the way he came alive when he told them. In fact he only seemed to be there, with us, when he told them.

Generally speaking, as long as I didn't cause too much trouble, I got along with my mother. I was walking on tippy-toe all the time. She bought me things, especially storybooks; she took me to play at an occasional friend's house, if she approved of the friend, but not until I was in first grade.

But before that, when the rage at being so constricted and restricted built up in me and I threw horrible tantrums, beating my head against the floor and screaming terrible screams that brought my grandmother running from the kitchen, it was only then my mother and father wondered about my behavior, wondered if anything was wrong. I never obviously disobeyed and they ignored most of what I did do, unless it reflected favorably on them, in which case I was lavishly praised. So these outbursts frightened them. They frightened me too because I couldn't stop once I started. It was only after I could catch my breath between sobs that I was able to get control. They were never able to offer anything to assuage my obvious suffering, suffering that surprised and shocked them every time.

The year before my brother was born I had to start kindergarten. It was boring. We didn't read. We made things and I was bad at making things with my hands. I botched making a hatchet out of cardboard for George Washington's birthday and had to sit and watch while everyone was pretending to chop down a cherry tree.

Every morning I would cry and nag, "I don't want to go. I want to stay home."

My mother said, "The truant officer will come for you."

"I don't care. Anything is better than kindergarten. I don't know any of the kids and they're not nice to me." I was remembering how they laughed when I couldn't make the hatchet.

My mother had asked my father to get me admitted to a school out of my district because my mother said it had a better reputation. One of the little things he could do as a precinct captain. Since I didn't live near the children I went to school with and they knew each other and lived near each other, I felt isolated, left out.

Some time around the year I began school my mother learned how to drive our car and she took me to school on bad days. In Chicago in the fall and winter, most of the days were bad. We stopped and picked up schoolmates along the way. She was running our private school bus. Maybe she drove me because she felt guilty about making me go to school so far from home. If she hadn't driven, I would have walked with the other children. I might have made some friends.

Maybe she drove me to keep me from getting sick which I did, a lot. I secretly thought she drove me to keep me from being too friendly with the girls and boys along the way. She could pick up the ones she liked, she could manage things in the car.

The only people I was allowed to play with at home were boys whose parents were friends of hers. I didn't get along with them because they were boys and didn't want to play with paper dolls. They tried to lure me into the basement, which scared me.

To stop my nagging about school my mother talked to the principal and I was admitted to first grade early because I could read and was learning to write.

Things were better in a hurry. My first grade teacher and I hit it off at once and my learning went even faster. I liked the students too. At recess I didn't have to stand around alone any more. Girls invited me to play baseball, hopscotch, or just came over to talk and be nice. I had people to eat lunch with. I made friends and was able to get my mother to take me to their houses to play after school, until she became pregnant and everything stopped.

Some of my school friends came over once in a while and we made up stories that we acted out with my paper dolls. Those times were the best, but they didn't happen often because my mother didn't like some of the girls and other times she was too sick to have "all that noise."

By then I was deep into reading Greek and Roman mythology in books for children we picked up on our frequent shopping trips for baby clothes. The brothers Grimm, Hans Christian Anderson and other famous authors as well. I branched off into the Bobbsey Twins and Nancy Drew and everything else I could get my hands on. I was the most frequent patron of my grade school library, reading through almost everything by the time I graduated from eighth grade. But by then I was racing through the collection at the local public library, carrying home stacks of books which I devoured and returned in a couple of days, and then picked up another batch.

I think reading and living in my imagination with my paper dolls was what carried me through those early years. I invented a rich world, stimulated by the books I read, filled with swashbuckling noblemen, glorified slaves, heroes and demons, witches and beautiful maidens, empowered children, happy homes, a well-populated, exciting world to which I retreated whenever reality became too rough. My father retreated, too, into his own world. Maybe I was more like him than I realized.

My baby brother was a constant accusing presence. I was scolded if I so much as touched him. He was my mother's sole preoccupation when she finally brought him home, making me feel invisible, replaced. At first he fascinated me, so small and noisy. I couldn't imagine my mother changing his dirty diapers, she had a horror of dirt or mess of any kind. But she changed him constantly, seeming to enjoy the process.

My parents called him Martin. Everyone else called him Marty. My mother smothered him with kisses and affection as I watched, unable to recall if she had ever treated me like that.

I was sharing the sleeping porch with Aunt Bernice by then, since Uncle George had moved out. Being roommates with her was the only positive thing that had happened to me in a while.

Marty was in my crib in my parents' bedroom, and my toy box was moved into the sleeping porch. I never played with the things in the box. Presents on my birthdays, objects I didn't care about. I had a small bookcase where my treasures, my books, were kept, next to my bed. I still had a secret stash of books behind the piano.

I loved to lie in bed and watch Aunt Bernice get ready to go to work in the morning. She left before I had to get up for school, first grade. She was beautiful and sweet and friendly and I adored her. She was like the big sister I never had. She made the bitter pill of the baby brother less hard to take. She showed me how she put on makeup, how it made her look even better, and she talked about her boyfriends.

She sat in front of a mirror she had set up on a dresser near her bed.

"See?" she said, holding up a long black pencil, "if I draw a line right here," she made a mark on her eyelid, "and right here," she drew lines under her eyes over the lashes, "see how much bigger it makes my eyes?"

She turned to show me. I was sitting up in bed, fascinated by this glimpse into an adult female world I had never seen. My mother used powder, rouge on her cheeks and lipstick. It took her one second to do the job.

Then Aunt Bernice showed me how she enhanced the color of her eyes, very blue, with shadow on her lids.

"Do your boyfriends like when you make up your face?" I asked, bemused at the prospect of all this. Making up my face? Coloring my eyelids? Without blue eyes, what color would I make them? My eyes were very dark, almost black.

"Oh, yes," Aunt Bernice said. "They always tell me how good I look. They never see me without makeup," she pointed, "like you do."

She had two boyfriends at the moment and they both wanted to marry her and she didn't know which one to choose. Would she let them see her without makeup first?

She put down her lipstick and laughed. "Oh, my. That would really wreck my chances!"

I didn't think so. She was beautiful with or without makeup. It was her personality and her sunny ways that made her so endearing.

These morning conversations made me feel very grown up, like I was living in one of the novels I had discovered in my parents' bookcase.

I lived in that apartment, went to school, and tried to get along. I didn't succeed very well.

Often I locked myself in the bathroom and shouted through the door as my mother pounded on the other side.

"You'll see!" I yelled. "I'll kill myself! I'll drink this bottle of iodine and die and you won't be able to torture me any more!"

I didn't know what else to do to express my frustration, my eight year old needs, my identity as a human being with thoughts and feelings that were mine and no one else's.

There wasn't much conversation or interacting among the family. When my mother and father talked about something important, they went into their bedroom and closed the door. Never witnessing adults handling conflict, I learned very little about how people dealt with hard things when I was young.

My mother's code seemed based entirely on what she wanted others to think about her and how she ran her family. I would hear her talking about someone I thought was a friend to another friend on the telephone and then hear her say something exactly opposite to my grandmother. Something not nice. So when she complimented me or praised me, I didn't believe her.

My mother scolded and punished. And I guess though I hated when she did those things, at least I accepted them as being true. I had a very low opinion of myself. I knew I was smart but that wasn't bringing me happiness, the circle of friends I wanted, or the freedom I craved.

My mother questioned me constantly until I ran into the dining room where she chased me around the table shouting, "Where were you yesterday after school? What were you doing? Who were you with?" Trying to catch me and make me confess. To what? Mass murder? Thinking for myself? Where I really was – at the library.

The thing was, I could outsmart them, everyone in the family. I was getting top grades in school. My father doted on me, gave me anything I wanted, except his attention. My teachers loved me. School was the only rewarding thing in my life.

My friends at school were becoming interested in boys, and so was I. I did everything they did, not really liking the boys but hoping for enlightenment. I was interested in the process, in finding out what "sex" was, the few inklings I had gained from overheard conversations and books I had read, not too edifying. The books my mother gave me on the subject were clinical, they described something I considered revolting, and though I asked questions, there were very few answers, my mother clearly too embarrassed to talk about the unmentionable subject.

I figured I didn't have a chance to be popular, the ultimate goal, given my looks. Boys didn't care about brains. They liked pretty girls. My mother curled my straight hair into little ringlets – it was my fault, I made her do it, anything to make me look different – and gave me dresses my grandmother made for me. To save money, my mother said.

My face had broken out early. I was eight, tall for my age. I towered over most of the boys who hadn't begun to grow yet. I was wearing glasses, so near-sighted I could hardly see across the dining room table. All that reading in the dark behind the piano had taken its toll. My mother said I had inherited Uncle Sammy's bad eyes. He was the only other one in the family who wore glasses.

As a way of countering my bad looks, I took up piano. Popular piano to make the boys take notice. Any lessons I wanted that were connected to music were all right with my parents. Even popular music. My mother objected briefly, but my father agreed, as usual, to anything I wanted.

My teacher was a peppy lady who taught me chords on the grand piano in our living room. I banged out the chords with my left hand, playing the tunes of popular songs with my right hand and sounding pretty good. I pretended I was Aunt Bernice sitting at the piano, thundering out the music.

I played at one of the school parties, my hair tightly curled but working hard to straighten out, my dress freshly made by grandma, its silky folds hanging on my skinny body, my glasses on my big nose, my pimples unsuccessfully covered by Aunt Bernice.

Everyone gathered around and clapped. I was feeling better about things when I heard one boy say, "She plays a mean piano, but did you see what she looks like?"

That was the end of my piano playing.

My school friends would get together in the evening, but I lived too far from everyone to be with them at night, so, aside from a few parties I was invited to, and a couple that my mother allowed me to give at home (after the second one, she vowed never again, too much noise, too much mess, popcorn everywhere), I spent the times after school and in the evenings alone.

When I wasn't reading, I listened to popular songs on the radio and my small portable phonograph, and was filled with romantic thoughts about love, having only what I had read to help me imagine what love would be like. I didn't believe the stories of my friends at school, since I couldn't imagine, at the age of ten, being in love with any of the boys around us. I imagined heroes, swashbucklers like the Three Musketeers, heroes from France and England and ancient Greece, make-believe characters to go along with my make-believe thoughts.

Grade school passed smoothly enough, academically anyway, but the time was marked by much illness. In the space of two years I contracted measles, scarlet fever and various respiratory infections, blamed on my tonsils, which were removed, with much fuss and ice cream and Jell-O. I missed a lot of school but my mother brought my homework for me to do when I wasn't too sick, and I managed to keep up.

By the time I reached eighth grade, Aunt Bernice had gotten married and moved out and the back sleeping porch was mine alone. It took a while to get used to sleeping by myself. I was sure the back of the house would catch fire at night and burn me up. That part of the building was made of wood, the front of the building was brick. I had nightmares and woke up screaming, "Mom! Mom! I'm burning! The house is burning!"

My mother came running in. "Nothing is burning, everything is safe, the house is not on fire." After a few nights of this, she became a little testy. When I called out the next night and she didn't answer, I told myself to grow up. I was almost in high school. The nightmares stopped.

Graduation came and, sadly, I moved on to high school. I hated to leave my teachers. They hugged me and kissed me and said to be sure to keep in touch. Most of my school friends – my only friends- were going to the high school in the district they lived in, so off I went on the bus, alone.

I look back on those early years and two emotions stand out – anger and fear. Anger at the restrictions and frustrations, fear at what I did not understand, which was just about everything.

Aunt Bernice

CHAPTER 7

MARTY

When my brother Marty started to get bigger and learned to walk he was very wild. I secretly enjoyed watching my mother chase after him as he ran away from her. I stayed back, not helping, even though I could run faster than both of them.

Finally, she bought a harness. I was outraged. Even though I couldn't stand him I thought treating him like a dog was awful. I tried to play with him to make him feel better but he didn't seem to mind the harness at all. He called it "horsie" and just yanked the handle out of my mother's hands and went tearing down the sidewalk, yelling, "Giddyupp!" with her running after him as I doubled over laughing on the sidewalk.

The more Marty grew, the more we clashed. I didn't let him play with my things or read my books. I rarely said anything nice to him. Or let him sit near me at the dinner table. Often he kicked me and I screamed and then he was in trouble.

I usually started a fight by saying something nasty, like "You smell bad," or "I hate you." Then he hurt me with a slap or a punch and I ran crying to my mother, and he was in more trouble.

With my mother bossing him and my grandmother telling him he couldn't do this or that, and me my usual mean self, Marty didn't have a chance. My father was at work all day and when he came home my mother told him about what my brother had done that day, like breaking a dish or a vase, talking back, coming home late after school, and we would have a battle at the dinner table every night, with my father trying to be judicious and my mother constantly accusing.

I sat at the table, unable to eat, the tension making my stomach hurt, but there was nothing I could do about anything. Marty was about eight, I was fourteen then, busy with my own life in high school. I could have told him how I handled things at home to get my way, but I didn't think he would listen, to me especially. His method of coping was total rebellion, making life miserable for him and everyone at the dinner table, which consisted of my mother, my father, my grandmother, Marty and me.

From time to time my father tried to change the subject. "Let me tell you about something interesting that happened —"

But my mother broke in. "Sam, you have to do something about Martin's behavior," and on and on until he gave up and the battle began anew.

Marty did poorly in school though he tested out as highly intelligent. I heard about him sporadically, my mother complaining, my father suffering silently. After a while Marty rarely showed up for dinner. I didn't blame him.

Marty's bad behavior really bothered my father. He cared about Marty and wanted to help him but didn't know how. I overheard whispered conversations between my mother and father about what to do about Marty.

"I don't know, I don't know," my mother repeated and my father shook his head and look sad. I didn't know either. I figured it out a long time afterward, when it was too late.

There was an invisible barrier between my father and Marty and me. It was like my father was afraid to tell us what he was really thinking. Afraid to get involved. Afraid he cared too much to be objective. That was the trouble. He was too objective, his feelings, what we wanted above all, at least I did, were always under tight control, my mother watching, making sure he didn't give in.

If it was something material, something my father could hand over, that was easy for him. It was the other things, the loving, the listening, the time spent with us, the caring that we missed. The stories he told at the table were, I think, his substitution for them. I think Marty missed a sense of being loved. He missed it more than I did. When he was small he was very sensitive to every voice tone, every word spoken. He would cry a lot, then pout, his lower lip way out, and walk away into a corner and stand there for a long time

When Marty grew older, he never bothered to attend school, ran with a delinquent crowd, and finally was sent to a school for difficult children when the local grade school kicked him out for smoking. He became an alcoholic in his teens, and bedeviled my parents with his addiction. My father tried his best to keep it a secret. He was very conscious of what people thought of him and our family. My father had long ago given up trying to find out why Marty acted the way he did.

Marty went to the country club where my father played golf with his friends and sat at the bar and drank until he was a nuisance. He ran up enormous bills. My father finally quit the country club. He was too embarrassed to belong.

Marty went through a series of marriages, one of the wives attacking him with a knife, and my father kept buying him out of marriages and other troubles all the years that Marty lived.

My father thought Marty needed a job, a place to go every day, so he bought a carpet business with Uncle Hy, his younger brother, and Marty and my cousin Freddie went to work there. Except Marty wasn't there very much. Marty and Freddie became friends and many years later, long after Marty had died, Freddie gave me a different picture of him.

"He was a happy-go-lucky guy," Freddie said. "Made friends easily and seemed to always have a good time. We got along fine.

Your mother wanted us to be friends so I would be a good influence." He laughed. "Marty was a lot of fun. We'd go out and drink and pick up girls and I would get in trouble because I was always coming home late. So my mother told me Marty was a bad influence on me." He was silent a moment.

"It was a shame, a waste of a smart, good-looking guy who people liked. He could have done something with his life. He needed a mentor, a guide to show him how to do the right thing. My mother showed me. My father was always too busy. Marty squandered his life, with nobody, he felt, on his side."

Marty didn't live very long. When he was in his forties, cirrhosis of the liver killed him. My father told everyone he died of pneumonia.

CHAPTER 8

MY FATHER'S FAMILY

My father came from a large family, four brothers and one sister. It seemed large to me, having only the one brother whom I tried to ignore. We didn't see my father's family very often, mostly because they lived in another part of Chicago. But when holiday time came around we would all get together at my paternal grandmother's apartment.

Grandma Bessie Allen was a short round woman with a kind face, a friendly smile and a bun of white hair at the nape of her neck. She was the classic matriarch. Her sons did whatever she asked of them, no matter the demands of their assorted wives.

I admired Grandma Bessie a lot. She was a gutsy woman. Despite being born in a foreign country, Russia, she knew how to get around Chicago better than I ever did. She would travel alone on streetcars to her different meetings, even after her sight left her and she was legally blind. In her eighties, she took a freighter, alone, to Israel and was caught in a terrible storm in the middle of the Atlantic. As she told it, it was very exciting. She didn't even get seasick.

Grandma Bessie practiced Orthodox Jewry, something the rest of the family did not do, but they respected her right to do so and would not ring her doorbell or call on the phone on Saturday, and one of my uncles or my aunt always came over and turned on her lights.

Holidays like Passover and Rosh Hashanah were happy times, all of us gathered around Grandma Bessie's table overflowing with food, all the Jewish goodies she loved to make. She would urge us to eat as much as possible. My mother nibbled disapprovingly at her plateful. She couldn't stand to be upstaged at these affairs, considering herself a better cook.

But my father -- he loved being with his brothers and sister. They sang and talked and had a wonderful time, reminiscing about the past, talking about some current event, and being a family together. The warmth was palpable, something I didn't experience often at home.

I haven't mentioned my Jewish upbringing, mostly because it was another stressful thing between my parents and myself. My father was the president of the synagogue and my mother the president of the synagogue sisterhood. They wanted me to go to Sunday school and be confirmed. I objected violently. There were only a few children in the Sunday school class and they were all boys, obnoxious boys, sons of my parents' friends who were members of the synagogue. Sometimes I felt like I was the only girl -- in the world.

I was duly confirmed, against my will, arguing every Sunday morning that I did not want to go to school, and vowed to myself that religion would never be a part of my life. Organized religion, that is. I did believe there was something more powerful than any human, which could supply answers to all the unexplained things happening in the world. When I was young I believed you could find the answers to anything if you looked long enough and hard enough.

My father's oldest brother, Ben, was a dentist, bluff and gruff and no-nonsense. He frightened me a little when I was very young. His daughter, my cousin Dellora, was the nearest to my age and we stayed glued together at these gatherings. We were a lot alike, having had much the same upbringing. Dominant mothers, younger brothers. In fact our mothers used to walk us side by side in our carriages when we were babies and their family came to visit, both mothers dressed in their nurses outfits with masks over their faces.

I liked these family gatherings because of all the commotion and camaraderie and because Del and I could get together and talk and giggle and nobody cared. The commotion was mostly caused by my boy cousins, Del's brother Murray, cousin Freddie, and my brother Marty. They crawled under the table and fooled around and no one could get them out. My mother would be enraged because my brother was misbehaving in public, though nobody knew how she felt but me. My mother couldn't stand any impropriety from us, especially in front of others.

My father was the next oldest brother. He started out as an accountant but then went to law school at night when I was small. He worked non-stop at his job for the city law department, trying to support us. His major ambition was to be noticed at City Hall and put on the ticket to become a judge. That's why he became a precinct captain and we lived where we did, so he could rise in the political hierarchy of Chicago. He didn't take into account the iron hand of Mayor Daley the First.

My Uncle Hy was the next brother. He was a dentist like his older brother Ben, but he kept breaking his arm -- the same arm -- in one accident after another. His doctor told him to get another profession or forget about using that arm. He went to night school and became an accountant, ending up as the comptroller of a large metal company.

My folks were socially friendly with Uncle Hy and Aunt Sophie, moreso than with the rest of my father's family. Their kids, Freddie and Margie, were younger than I was but they were a lot of fun, lively and loving and I liked being around them. They cheered me up, made me feel as though every family group in our family wasn't the same as mine. We saw more of them when Aunt Sophie's sister and her family moved into a house not far from our apartment.

There were barbecues at the Terry's, Aunt Sophie's relatives, every summer, where we always had a great time. The Terrys were big kidders, playing practical jokes and making fun of everything. My father was in a constant state of glee, laughing a lot at what everyone said. Even my mother giggled at the merriment.

They served up huge dinners, chickens, steaks, hot dogs and hamburgers, all the trimmings and we ate, even I ate, until we were ready to burst. Huge slabs of watermelon would top off the meal and then we waited for the Good Humor Man and his truck to come by for the best treat of all.

My father's next brother, Phil, was quiet and kept to himself. Many thought he was the most brilliant, a linguist. He had a disease that made him lose all his hair and he wore a terrible wig. I guess that was why he was so self-conscious. Too bad he didn't live in the 21st century where bald is beautiful.

In World War II he was a translator and one day was invited up on a reconnaissance mission from England, where he was stationed, into Germany. He was shot down over the English Channel in 1944. It was a sad gathering the day we came together at Grandma Bessie's after Uncle Phil was posthumously awarded the Silver Star. She held it in her hand, sitting on a low stool, tears streaming down her face, and kept asking why? Why?

The next brother, Uncle Nate, was the playboy of the family. He dated chorus girls and all kinds of society cuties. When he decided to get married, Del and I were all adither. Grandma was having a dinner and we were invited to meet the bride.

"What do you think she looks like?" I said to Del, sitting next to me on Grandma's couch. I was twelve, she was thirteen.

"I'll bet she's gorgeous," Del replied, "with beautiful clothes and long blonde hair. Lots of makeup too."

"I wish they'd get here. I can't wait to see her." I fidgeted in my seat with impatience.

Then the bride-to-be and her family arrived with a flurry of hugs and kisses from the aunts and uncles and Grandma Bessie, who didn't care what she looked like just so Uncle Nate was getting married, at last, and the girl was Jewish.

When we saw her we couldn't believe it. She was pretty enough but, to our eyes, gigantic, almost taller than our uncle, not fat but large, very large. Her mother was stunning, slender, beautiful and elegantly dressed.

Del and I sat across the table from the new family member-to-be, not able to keep our eyes off her. She didn't say much, or smile much, or respond much. We knew there had to be something about her that had attracted Uncle Nate, whom everyone said was a connoisseur of women. Maybe, we whispered, when we get to know her, we'll find out.

My father put Uncle Nate through law school and helped him get started in a law practice. Uncle Nate didn't work very hard, always the playboy.

"He doesn't have to work hard," my mother whispered. "His wife's family is very wealthy."

He was elected to the board of one of the local racetracks and gained some prominence in the city. All this time my father was practicing law in the torts division at City Hall, in his quest for a judgeship.

Aunt Sara was my father's youngest sibling, the only girl in the family, and the one I related to the most. She went to the University of Chicago, was brilliant and interested in anything in the arts and sciences. She married young and divorced early. When she married again, she had a child, a little boy, but her husband was tragically killed in an auto accident. After some time, when her son was older, she went back to school and earned a master's degree in speech therapy at Northwestern University.

While she was studying there, she met the curator of rare books at the library and they were eventually married. He was Viennese, very cultured and a poet, who later gained renown in poetry circles. His name was Felix Pollak. He kissed our hands at all family occasions. I thought that was very continental. My mother disapproved. As a child it seemed to me, my mother frowned on all forms of affection.

My aunt was successful as a speech therapist, doing work for the city of Evanston. When her husband was asked to be the curator of rare books at the University of Wisconsin at Madison, they moved and continued their careers. She earned a PHD when she was 88 and is still living and working and going to concerts in her middle 90's.

Actually, she celebrated her 95th birthday in November 2004.

All my father's brothers died in their nineties, except Uncle Phil. My father was 90 when he died, my mother 93. But the one who took the prize for living the longest, most illustrious life was Uncle George, my mother's brother, who died at 103.

Many years later, after I read Gabriel Garcia Marquez's book, "One Hundred Years of Solitude," with the empty graveyard, I thought of my family, living far beyond anyone's expectations, both sides living longer than their friends, having only one another and their younger spouses. And myself and my cousins. But it was in relation to myself, my genetic inheritance, that I thought about their longevity and what it meant, especially about Uncle George touching three centuries. It gave me the shivers.

The Allens, my father in the top corner.

CHAPTER 9

HIGH SCHOOL

When I was thirteen I started high school, insisting to my mother that I wanted to take the bus alone my first day. She was all set to drive me.

I was afraid she would come into the school and start arranging my schedule. I knew the high school was very large, much larger than the grammar school where I had been comfortable, more at home than in my home, but I was determined to meet this new challenge on my own.

There were a few older students on the bus I knew from grammar school. They smiled and nodded, not getting too close to the skinny freshman with armloads of supplies. My mother had made sure I had everything, more than everything.

As I settled in my seat near the window, squeezing as far over as I could, my lap loaded with books, notebooks, pens and boxes, I felt as though I was wrapped in invisible plastic from head to toe. Nothing was coming in, nothing was going out. I felt hopelessly unready for what was before me, academically, socially, and every other way.

Would I be able to handle the new surroundings, the new girls and boys? Would I be able to make friends, would I be popular?

As I watched Chicago neighborhoods pass by the bus window, fear took over. Some girls had jobs at thirteen. They belonged to clubs after school, went to parties, went out with boys, went downtown on the streetcar with their friends. That was unknown territory to me.

The school loomed up in my window, enormous, Gothic, with pointed arches over the windows and doors. I juggled my books and supplies to get out my instructions, pushed through the crowds of students in the hall to the home room number on my list, after asking the way from hall guards posted along the way. I was assigned a locker and, with relief, put everything inside and locked it with the combination lock I had brought. I had spent the whole day before practicing how to open it.

In home room I sat next to a couple of girls who introduced themselves.

"Hi! You're new around here, aren't you?" said Joan, tall and thin with black hair and a nice smile.

"I am new. I went to Darwin in a different district but I'm happy to be here," not exactly meaning it.

"Welcome!" Esther smiled, holding out a hand. "It's nice to meet a newcomer." She was chubby, as short as I was.

I smiled for the first time in weeks and could feel the invisible plastic wrap starting to unravel. We went off to our first classes, happily they were the same, and I was introduced to high school, eagerly looking forward to what it had in store. With friends, you could handle anything, I thought.

I didn't look too different from the other freshmen. Our bewildered looks and our frequent wrong turns in the hall gave us away. I had insisted that my mother let my hair alone and it was pushed back and turned under by itself. I had insisted that my mother take me shopping for skirts and sweaters and I was dressed like everyone else. My main idea was to blend in with the crowd. I wanted to learn, unnoticed, a little about how high school worked. And so far it was okay.

That first day we went to abbreviated classes, running through our schedules so we would know what to do the next day, the first real day of school. Esther and Joan waved goodbye as I climbed on the bus to go home for lunch, feeling exhilarated by my new surroundings and my new friends. We made a date to meet the next morning.

When I reached my bus stop, near the local library, I stopped to pick up something to read, and though I had left everything I had brought to school in my locker, I opened the apartment door -- I now had my own key-- loaded down again, this time with books I planned to read that day and night. I was reading mysteries, as a change from historical romances, as many as I could carry home at one time. I liked to play the game of guessing the murderer before the author told me who it was.

Sometime during the first week of school I walked into the offices of the newspaper, to try and get a job, step number one in my secret plan. My ambitions were high. I would graduate as editor. I would go on to greater fame. I would be unstoppable. My friend Joan wanted to work on the paper too. Her boyfriend was already on the staff so she was hired at once. I thought, a little jealously, she doesn't want to work here to write, she just wants to be near her boyfriend, whereas I was a bona fide candidate.

It took that whole first year. I had to get friendly with the journalism teacher before I was able to work on the paper. You had to do well in freshman English to qualify. Luckily she was my freshman English teacher. I wrote as many essays and papers as I could squeeze in -- it was my first taste of the need for clout. Joan was established on the paper before I was appointed, by the journalism teacher, not the editor. The teacher usually didn't interfere, but she liked me and wanted me to succeed. The newspaper became my main and only interest.

Social life came before work for most of my schoolmates. There were hops in the school gym at lunchtime, and Joan and Esther dragged me. I was still conscious of my looks, though I had filled out in the right places by then and didn't resemble a scarecrow. I noticed what everyone wore and I tried to wear things that would make me look good. Some of the girls used makeup. But my complexion was still iffy and I was afraid to try.

I could just visualize the scene at home if I walked in wearing makeup!

Mother: "Elaine! What is that on your face? Don't you want your complexion to *ever* clear up?"

Grandma: "Painting her face! What do they teach in that school?"

I was afraid to try a lot of things, though I did at my friends' urging, like having lunch at the little store across the street from the school, where all the popular kids ate. The boys hung around, some smoked, a lot of them were on the football team. They were huge and scared me. My friends thought I was crazy.

We were sitting at the counter one winter day at lunch and I had just blown off another football player with one of my patented dirty looks. I was a freshman and not supposed to act that way.

"Elaine," Joan said, "what's wrong with you? These guys are nice. Look, they like you. If you'd only pay a little attention to them, I bet one of them would ask you out."

"I don't want to go out with them. We don't have anything in common."

"How do you know if you don't even answer when they say something to you?" Esther said.

"Okay, okay. I'll talk to them." I couldn't risk losing my two best friends over a dumb thing like football boys.

They both had boyfriends and decided, "Okay, from now on, our main occupation is finding a boyfriend for you."

Lotsa luck, I thought.

I concentrated on getting the best grades I could that first year. It wasn't hard. I had built a background of knowledge with my reading habits, so I seemed to know everything everyone else was just learning. The standards of the Chicago school system were not the highest. If you handed in your homework and showed up for class you were automatically in the top class group.

Things were brewing overseas. It was 1939 and there was a rumbling crossing the ocean where Germany was on the move.

My mother and father looked concerned, my grandmother worried. She remembered the pogroms in Russia and made pronouncements about us all being massacred that we pooh-poohed.

I could not imagine what war would be like. I questioned my parents about World War One but, as usual, they didn't want to worry me. So with their evasiveness they scared me instead. I listened to the radio as much as I could, concentrating on the news broadcasts from overseas. President Roosevelt was God in our house and he could do no wrong. Everyone placed their faith in him, sure that he would protect the people of the country from catastrophe.

I tried to push what was going on in the rest of the world into a corner to make room for what was happening in my life. School, the newspaper, the girls and the boys were taking up a lot of time. Esther and Joan kept fixing me up with dates, mostly from the football team. They insisted that those were the best, the most sought-after boys. My father objected violently to my going out with any of them, but after meeting a few, and after I pleaded, he decided they were harmless and gave in, as usual.

I was determined to fit in, but to me, those football boys seemed like big dumb elephants. Especially on Saturday night, after a football game. My date was so tired that he could hardly walk or talk. On one date, we all went to a movie and my date was asleep almost before the movie started. Joan and Esther were cuddling with their boyfriends in the dark and were so busy they didn't even watch the movie.

I sat there alone and wondered if dating was always like this. I was a sophomore by then and it seemed I should be having a better time. My date finally woke up and put his arm around me. I moved away. He would have to be a lot more attentive than that. Then I heard him snoring. The end.

We had a monosyllabic conversation on the way home. Mostly I nodded and shrugged. He talked about the game that day and how well he had played. I yawned.

When we were at my front door after the date, he tried to kiss me goodnight. Fat chance. I wouldn't be asked out again by him or any of his friends and that saved me the embarrassment of making up an excuse to say no. My father applauded my good sense. But word got around that I was "stuck up."

The newspaper office was the only place I was happy. Classes became something to be gotten through. I did the work and looked out the window. But on the newspaper I wrote stories, helped with the paper's layout and rewrote most of Joan's offerings when she asked.

There were a couple of boys on the paper more interesting than the usual run of males, Stuart and Joe, but they were so unattractive physically, I couldn't raise my interest level. They were not in the same class with Athos, Porthos or Aramis.

But they were nice to talk to. They were worried about being drafted. They hated to leave high school. Joe was thinking about lying about his age.

We were standing around the journalism office waiting for our next classes.

"You can't do that," I exclaimed. "They'd catch you and throw you in jail."

"Just kidding." Joe gave me a nudge with his elbow.

"Look." Stuart was reading the CHICAGO TRIBUNE, searching the morning news for a story idea.

"How about if we write a story about one of our graduates who's in the news? Maybe just entering the service. You know, human interest about someone everyone knows and remembers. We could interview his mother for details."

"Good idea," Joe said. "Let's see that section."

I had a class and had to leave, as the two of them hunched over the paper, discussing possibilities.

About this time I started getting wild crushes on perfect strangers I would see as I rode the bus or as I walked along the street. Usually they were tall, well built, with black curly hair and, I imagined, blue eyes. Usually a crooked grin.

One afternoon on the bus on the way home from school I spotted a sailor, lanky in his whites, his hat at a rakish angle, ambling down the street, a broad smile on his face, a dimple in his chin. I practically swooned and ran to the telephone as soon as I was home to call up Joan and Esther and tell them all about it, making sure my grandmother was not on telephone watch.

We giggled a lot and Joan said, "Good, at least you're getting interested and maybe one day one of these Romeos will walk into your life." Esther said, "We'll be upperclassmen next year, juniors, and will have even more people to date. Even college men."

That really terrified me.

In the middle of this, Pearl Harbor happened. My family and I were listening to the radio when President Roosevelt gave his "day of infamy" speech. We had to wait for the afternoon paper to see pictures of the horror. Newsreels at the movies were full of the attack. The country started mobilizing. We were at war.

It was hard to care about things at school while the world was blowing up. Since I was usually afraid of most things I couldn't control, I lived in a constant state of fear no one knew about. The older boys started disappearing from school. They enlisted or were drafted. The war news went from bad to worse. The country was gearing itself into a giant armament factory. But we weren't winning quickly as the politicians said we would. The battles in the South Pacific were going badly. We had forgotten how to wage war. Then new generals took over and things began to change. We got the hang of it and were more successful.

Germany was another story. The radio broadcasts of Hitler ranting to the cheering masses made me feel like a trap had opened up under my feet and I was about to fall in. Though I couldn't understand what he was saying, he put me in a constant state of terror. I had nightmares again, this time about war.

Back at school, aside from the shortage of boys, things went on as if there was nothing unusual happening. We went to parties, out on dates. Proms were coming up. Everyone was shopping for a dress, a date, a party to go to. I went along, not knowing what else to do. My dates, everyone's dates, were the younger boys, some even shorter than I was. One boy, Sheldon Katz, was really persistent. He asked me out constantly. He was short but very smart in school. He had a blond crew cut and wore sloppy clothes and talked about books a lot. I liked that. Finally I said yes and he came to my house to pick me up. I was happy to see he looked neat that night.

My father gave the poor kid the third degree. Where were we going? What time would we get back? What were his intentions? God! We were fifteen years old. I almost died of embarrassment. My mother went into a dither, fussing about what I would wear, driving me nuts about my hair, my clothes. I decided it wasn't worth it, especially since I was pining over my latest crush, that gorgeous sailor I had seen from the bus. The date was okay. We went to a movie and then for a soda and he brought me home on the el and a streetcar by 10 o'clock, my father's deadline. It wasn't easy because we had to rely on the erratic schedules of the Chicago Transit system.

All during high school I kept up my habit of going to the local library, especially on warm nights, when I walked through the park and visited with the boys and girls who hung out there. I struck up an acquaintance with one of the boys who was older and not in the Army yet. We talked about books, the war, things that interested us. Sometimes he walked me home and carried my load of books. He was a senior, his name was Sam, not tall and gorgeous, but really nice.

One night as we chatted at my door, he asked, "Would you like to go out with me?" He had a friend and wondered if I knew someone and we could double date. I immediately thought of my cousin Del. She was the only girl I knew, besides me, who wasn't going steady.

We fixed it up for the following Saturday night. We would all go downtown to a movie and Del would sleep over at my house that night. I was very excited. I had never been downtown on a date. Del arrived - her father drove her - and we had to listen to her mother giving us instructions over the phone. She was even pickier than my mother and was afraid to let Del out of her sight. "Don't get home late." "Call me as soon as you get back from the date," and on and on. My father gave it to us from my end. "Be careful." "Don't talk to strangers." "Get home on time." It was a wonder I ever went out at all.

Finally the boys picked us up and off we went with my grandmother looking worried but thank goodness not saying anything. My parents had already gone to a dinner party, my father reluctantly. He wanted to give last minute orders, even though he knew Sam, the boy from the park. The boy's parents belonged to the synagogue so he was considered okay.

We rode the streetcars and els and had a lot of fun. There was so much to talk about. My date's friend and Del hit it off at once and we laughed and talked and forgot about the time.

"Gosh, Elaine," Del said. "I can't believe they let us do this. Actually go downtown alone on a date."

"Hey," Bernie, her date, said. "You're not alone. What are we, ghosts?"

"It's not you," I said. "It's our parents. They never let us do anything. You'd think we were made of glass, the way they treat us. This date is a miracle."

"I always wanted to be part of a miracle," my date Sam said. He looked out the window. "Here's our stop. Let's get on with this miracle."

Walking down the el steps, we laughed and held on to each other.

We saw a great movie, "Here Comes Mr. Jordan," a first run at the Chicago Theatre, and then walked down State Street, looking in store windows and stopping for things to eat. We climbed the el stairway to wait for a train to take us back, talking about the movie. We all liked it and felt sorry for Robert Montgomery. Nobody had a watch and we had no idea what time it was. The trains were slow and we transferred a few times, each time waiting it seemed like hours on the station platform. As the last train approached, we saw the sun coming up in the east.

When I put the key in my door, my mother yanked it open, wearing her angriest look and started right in. "Where have you been? Do you know how many times Dellora's mother has called? How do you think that makes us look?" Always her first thought.

Right behind her was my father looking me over to see if I showed signs of being molested. My grandmother was behind him, her face a knot of worry. I can imagine what she had to listen to while I was gone.

My mother said to Del, "Call your mother. Right away." She did and a few minutes later left the phone crying.

"What did she say?" I asked, almost afraid to find out. I had waited for her to get off the phone in the hall while my parents and grandmother went into the living room.

Del was sobbing but she said, "My mother called you a spoiled brat and said I could never sleep over again. She said she should have known you couldn't get a good upbringing in the neighborhood you live in."

I was outraged. I didn't dare tell my parents and start a feud. Things were bad enough. Del's parents were on the way to pick her up. They wouldn't let her sleep at my house for one minute.

When they arrived we told them we had spent most of the night waiting on el platforms for trains that were always late. They huffed and my aunt said we should have been more aware of what time it was. We agreed and apologized profusely but said we had been having such a good time talking that we forgot to notice. However my reputation was ruined forever with Del's parents.

My parents forbade me to go out with my friend Sam again but we met in the park whenever I went to the library. I guess you could say he was my first boyfriend and I found him all by myself.

Sometimes I would let him kiss me goodnight when he walked me home. I felt really grown up and finally in control of things. He didn't look like one of my crushes but he was there, a real person, and he liked me, and that was just fine.

During this time, my sophomore year, I used to dream in bed late at night while I listened to Dave Garroway on the radio. I loved his soothing voice, his low-key style. He played all the good music, big bands, Frank Sinatra. "That Old Black Magic" would send me into a tailspin. I guess I had a wild crush on Sinatra too. He wasn't good looking like my other crushes but he had great cheekbones, and that voice!

I never told a living soul how I really felt about things, what I wanted, how I planned to go about getting those things. There was no one I could confide in who would understand anything I was saying. My mother and father had their preconceived ideas about what young girls should think and do. I talked and giggled with my friends but they didn't have a clue about who I really was, what I really liked or wanted. Maybe I could have talked to Aunt Bernice or Aunt Sara or even Uncle George but they lived far from me, I seldom saw them and when I did it was in a family setting and there were too many people around for me to get one-on-one with any of them.

I refused to admit that I was like every other teenager, as I dreamed impossible dreams and hoped impossible hopes. I listened to the Hit Parade every week. Usually I was home. I didn't have a lot of dates, mostly because of my "stuck up" reputation, but also because I lived far from the high school and it was hard to pick me up.

My father Samuel as a child

CHAPTER 10

CANADA

In the summer of my sophomore year, my parents bought a new car, a shiny black Chevy with four doors, and they decided we would all take a trip.

"A driving trip!" my mother exclaimed, her eyes shining, full of excitement. I knew she really loved to drive.

My father said, "Where would you like to go, hon?"

She thought a minute, but I knew she knew the answer and just wanted to prolong the suspense.

"What about Canada?" she finally said. "I've always wanted to go there. They say the scenery is gorgeous, all those mountains and lakes. We could make stops along the road, and visit Ottawa, the capital, and Toronto, and if we have time, maybe even Montreal."

My father looked doubtful. "That's a lot of ground to cover. I only have a two week vacation."

My mother frowned a little. She didn't like to be stopped from doing what she wanted. I guess we were a lot alike in that respect.

"Since we're driving," she said, "we can make our own time frame, only go where we can in the time we have. Would that be all right with you?"

My father smiled, relieved. "That would be just fine."

He turned to Marty and me, sitting in the sunroom opposite our parents, Marty still around after dinner, on a couch across from the radio. The dinner had been better than most, the meat tender, the dessert, one of my grandmother's famous coffeecakes.

"What do you think, Elaine and Martin? Would you like to take a trip to Canada?"

We looked at each other. We had declared a temporary truce, almost getting along. I was fourteen, he was eight and getting bigger by the minute. I figured I'd better make peace before he was big enough to kill me.

"Who would drive?" I asked. My father tended to let his mind wander, going through red lights, stop signs and other traffic controls. My mother always drove too fast for conditions.

"We both would!" my mother exclaimed, delighted at the apparent solution to the problem, assuming we would agree it was a wonderful idea.

I imagined Marty and me in the back seat. How would we survive, even if we lived through the driving perils?

My father broke into my thoughts. "Well, children. What's your answer?"

Like we had a choice.

I said, "I would like to see something of the world. I've read a lot about Canada. It seems like a friendly, beautiful place, a good way to spend part of the summer."

My mother beamed. My father nodded.

"It's okay," Marty broke in, wanting to be part of the decision, which was already made.

Then I thought, the four of us are going to be together non-stop for two whole weeks. Just like a real family. We can talk about the things we see and experience, exchange ideas and get to know what we are really like. I began to get interested. Maybe it wouldn't be so bad after all. Maybe we would get to really like each other.

My father had the maps, my mother had the bags of food and the trunk was packed with our suitcases. We were each allowed one case. Luckily the new car had a large trunk, able to fit four cases neatly. My father enthused about the amount of room we had. I hadn't seen him so happy in a long while.

"This is going to be a great vacation," he announced solemnly. I said a silent amen.

There was a small discussion about who would be the first to drive. My father said he knew the way out of the city better than my mother so she agreed to let him begin the trip.

"I'll be the navigator for the first leg," she said, maps spread out in her lap.

My brother and I entered the car through opposite doors. He put down the seat divider between us and got his comic books out of his bag.

This was going to be better than I had hoped, assuming he had enough comics to take us through the entire journey.

My grandmother came downstairs to wish us a safe trip.

"Don't worry about me," she said. "Sammy and George will look in on me and I'll take care of the house while you're gone. I'll talk to Bernice every day." After she married, Aunt Bernice had moved to the South Side.

My father started to sing a song as we turned out of our street onto the boulevard that would take us to the highway. "Merrily we roll along –"

We all joined in. Even Marty looked up from his comics to lend his soprano voice. I was feeling better and better until my father ran a stop sign on the way to the highway ramp. Luckily no one was coming in the opposite direction.

"Dad?" I said. "Did you see that sign?"

No answer.

"Dad?" I shook his shoulder.

"What? What?"

My mother gave me a look. "Let your father concentrate on his driving, Elaine."

I muttered, "If he only would."

"What?" my mother said sharply.

"Nothing, nothing," I answered. Marty grinned at me and went back to his book.

I wished that I could read too. But reading in a moving vehicle made me carsick and I didn't want to throw up on our new car. I had a stash of books to read when we stopped overnight.

The drive was uneventful after that. The highway wasn't crowded and we tooled along at the speed limit. One good thing about my father's driving. He didn't speed. My mother was starting to fidget.

We snacked, ate sandwiches for lunch, sang and looked out the window, reading the Burma Shave signs out loud. We spotted different kinds of cars and yelled out the names. My brother had given up the comic books briefly to join in. Then we had to stop for gas and go to the bathroom. At the station my mother said she would drive until we stopped for dinner. My father moved to the passenger seat and promptly fell asleep. It was about two in the afternoon.

My mother settled herself in the driver's seat, there were no seat belts or air bags then, and adjusted her sunglasses. It was a beautiful sunny day, perfect for a drive, she said.

I looked at her as she shifted into the driving gear. There was a maniacal look on her face as she floored the gas pedal. We took off like a shot. My father woke up, startled.

"The speed limit is 55 miles an hour, hon," he said mildly. "We shouldn't go too fast breaking in a new car."

"Don't worry, I know what I'm doing," she said between gritted teeth and roared down the middle of the road like she was racing in the Indianapolis 500.

Marty let out a yell, "Yahoo!" and waved his comic book around like he was riding a bronco.

I grabbed the armrest under my window and held on. The scenery sped past so fast I couldn't read the signs that told where we had been and where we were going.

"Dad," I shouted, tapping his shoulder. "You've got the maps. Where are we?"

He fumbled with the pile of maps in his lap and opened up the one for the upper United States. "Let's see now. I wonder if we can make Detroit by dinnertime?"

"That's Michigan, Dad." At the speed we were traveling, I figured we'd be across the Canadian border by sundown.

The trip passed without an accident or a speeding ticket, thank goodness, and we reached our first stop for the night, on the border of Indiana and Michigan, hungry, tired, grimy and as for myself, numb with the terror that was mounting with every mile of near misses, passed turnoffs, u-turns into oncoming traffic to get back on the right roads. My father had dozed through it all, waking now and then to tell my mother to slow down, which she did until he went back to sleep.

Next morning my father took over the driving, bright and rested and alert.

Hooray, I thought, a respite from the breakneck pace. Maybe I could see some scenery along the way. It was warm and sunny, the sky spotted with high white clouds, a little breeze blowing through the open windows. We were heading due north, had passed through Illinois, part of Indiana, going around Lake Michigan and were on our way to Detroit.

I had had trouble sleeping the night before, my stomach in knots from anxiety but I didn't say anything because everyone was in high spirits at breakfast in the hotel coffee shop, looking forward to crossing into Canada and the real scenery.

"Do you think we'll see some Mounties?" Marty said, crunching his cereal.

"Probably," my father answered, as he sipped his coffee and looked over the morning newspaper.

"How far is it to the mountains?" I asked.

"I'll look at the map when we get to the car," my mother responded. "It shouldn't be too far."

As we cruised along the highway, my mother scanned the map

of Canada, pointing out to me the ragged lines where the mountains began. She was being so agreeable and friendly that I almost forgot her turn to drive was coming up soon. Maybe the high speeds at which she drove were cooling down her usual uptight ways.

More gas was needed, we stopped and the changing of the drivers took place. Tearing across Michigan, we arrived in Detroit in record time, took a city bypass and before we could catch our collective breath we were at the border. Marty was ecstatic. Mounties in their red uniforms and wide-brimmed hats were manning the border, their horses tethered nearby. Marty asked one of the Mounties for his autograph on a comic book. The Mounty obliged with a smile.

"Gosh! Will you look at that!" Marty held out the book to me so I could see the signature, a scrawl I couldn't read.

"That's really super," I said. "A real souvenir of the trip."

"Yeah," Marty said proudly. "My first."

Once across into Canada we set our course for Toronto where we planned to spend a couple of days before heading for Ottawa. There were a lot of small towns along the way with speed limits that cramped my mother's style.

"I can't believe we're supposed to go thirty miles an hour here," she grumbled.

"Would you like me to drive now?" my father asked. He had awakened at the border and was watching the passing scenery with interest.

"No, no," she said hurriedly, "I can manage. You just watch where we're going on the map so we don't get lost."

The terrain was changing, it was getting hilly and the roads were getting narrower. Once we were away from the towns, we started to climb sharply upward. The car was straining. My mother kept shifting gears to get the most speed. It was getting steeper every mile.

"Hon, slow down. You'll burn out something and we're not near anywhere."

She screeched around a corner and suddenly we were at a sheer drop, nothing below us but a few trees. She slammed on the brakes and the car shuddered and then slowed to a stop a few feet from the edge.

I was sitting on the front of my seat, hanging on to anything, the seat back, the food bags, even Marty, whose eyes were wide with terror at the sight.

"God, Mom!" he said. "That was a close one."

My father got out of the car. He came over to the driver's side and opened the door.

"My turn," he said. My mother moved away from the wheel without a word. She was as white as the clouds overhead and her hands were shaking.

The rest of the trip to Toronto went without incident. My father had apparently been shocked to attention because he stopped at all signals and turned at all the right intersections until we reached our hotel. My mother didn't say much. Marty and I started a game of War with some cards he took from his bag.

Toronto was fun. We walked around for a few days and saw all the sights. I was so happy I didn't have to get back into that car I skipped around smiling and enjoyed everything we did. The family noticed my good humor and my father remarked that the change of scenery was benefiting my disposition. I thought that was pretty funny but didn't say anything. I knew that very soon the Trip of Terror, as I now thought of our vacation, would begin again, and we'd be hurtling over mountains even taller and steeper than the hills we had just crossed.

My father had reserved rooms for us at hotels along our route. In Toronto we had one large room with two double beds and one attached bath. My mother and I slept in one bed, Marty and my father in the other. Nobody seemed to mind the close quarters and it turned out just fine.

I was particularly interested in the way my mother and father got along. They seemed to really love each other, and treated each other with consideration and respect. No overt sign of their feelings, like a kiss or a significant look passed between them, although a lot of hugs were exchanged between us all. It made me feel good that there was so much good feeling among us. There seemed to be so little at home.

Our times together at the restaurants were spent discussing the food and the sights we were seeing, our tours around the city filled with beautiful parks, buildings, friendly people and landmarks we discussed freely. Nothing personal came up, nothing to make any one of us uncomfortable. Marty, especially, seemed to be having a great time. He was easier to be with than he had ever been. I almost liked him.

Then it was time to leave Toronto if we were going to see Ottawa, the capital, with Parliament buildings just like London. I had seen a picture in one of the books I had read before we left.

We packed up and bought more supplies for the drive, since it seemed a long and hilly trip and we didn't want to waste time stopping on the way. My father filled up the car with gas and took a couple of extra cans of gas which he stored somewhere in the trunk, "in case we run short," he said.

The weather was cooler here but sunny and mild, with a nice breeze through the open windows. I settled back, telling myself the drive would be better, the mountains would be steep, and my mother would have to go slow or kill us all.

My father was first to drive, as usual, threading his way through Toronto traffic to the road out of town, watching traffic signals closely. I guess he didn't feel as at home here and couldn't daydream comfortably while driving.

The scenery was spectacular. Little lakes nestled in the mountains which rose above us, their peaks out of sight. The road narrowed, traffic was sparse, and we wound around and around, climbing to the top of the road and turning sharply to descend a little before going up again. We looked out at the range, spread to the horizon, mountaintops wreathed in clouds, the taller ones snow-capped.

After lunch we pulled over at a turnaround carved out of the mountain - there were many of these along the road – and my parents switched seats again. My mother climbed into the driver's seat and there was that maniacal look on her face again. Oh, no.

As soon as my father sat down he was asleep, not even waking as my mother screeched onto the road.

"Mom," I said, my stomach already in a knot, "this is dangerous territory here. If you look down, you can't see the bottom."

"I'm not looking down," she said. "I'm watching the road."

I sat back, my eyes closed, not wanted to look out the window, feeling us accelerate as we climbed, the gears shifting madly. We were going around and around and I was getting dizzy. I opened my eyes and looked at Marty. He was hanging on with both hands, panic on his face and I glanced at the speedometer.

"Mom! You're going ninety!"

My mother glanced at the gauge and slowed a little as we came to the top of the mountain and started down. She shifted to a lower gear, the brakes screeched as we picked up speed and she tried to control things. My father woke up and saw what was happening.

"Hon. Slow down. You can't go faster than 25 or 30 miles an hour here. Didn't you see the sign?"

She didn't answer but pumped the brakes until we slowed and coasted down the hill.

As we came into more populated terrain, with a few scattered houses, a large bumblebee flew in the open window.

Marty yelled, "A bee! A bee!" He started slapping at it with his comic book.

My mother was trying to concentrate on the driving, as Marty was hollering and jumping and swatting, making a huge commotion.

I started screaming, ducking the flying comic book and the bee, "It's going to sting us all! We have to get out!"

My father turned around and saw the bee buzzing around the back seat. It landed on a peach pit on the seat, then took off again.

"Hon, stop the car. There's a turnoff just ahead."

We were starting to climb again, the mountain hugging the road on one side, a sheer drop on the other.

My mother pulled over, Marty opened the door and before we could get out, the bee flew out the open door. I think he was as frightened as we were.

Marty flung himself back into his seat, slammed the door and closed the window. "We don't need that much fresh air," he said.

We continued over the mountains, my mother driving slower, my father watching closely, and I leaned back, completely exhausted from the fright, the bee, the ride, the whole vacation.

I couldn't figure out how my mother gave an impression of total lady-ness, quiet, cultured, intelligent, even sweet, to her friends, but when she was behind the wheel of a car she turned into a maniac race-car driver. She morphed – like Dr. Jekyll into Mr. Hyde.

We arrived in Ottawa that evening, had dinner and collapsed into our beds. Next day we toured but came back to the hotel early and decided we had better leave for home the next day or my father wouldn't get back to work on time. We had had enough.

We found an easier, less mountainous route home and arrived on the Sunday before my father had to report back to work. I never thought I would be glad to see that apartment, but I jumped into my bed before dark and cuddled under the covers, happy to be alive, amazed to have survived our family vacation.

CHAPTER 11

TRAUMA

My junior year began with Joan's boyfriend being named editor-in-chief. He was a senior and he would have the final say about who took the editorial jobs when he left. Everyone but I assumed the editor-in-chief in our senior year would be Claire, a quiet, very bright, not too friendly girl who worked on the paper as the editorial assistant to the main person, Joan's boyfriend. She was also the journalism teacher's special friend and helper. She was not interested in the social scene, never went out with boys, did not attend the school dances and wore unstylish clothes.

Joan thought, with her special clout, she would be editor-in-chief. She magnanimously offered me the feature editor's page if she was made editor. I tried not to smile as I accepted. There wasn't a prayer that she would get the job. Maybe if I had been more attentive to the journalism teacher after she put me on the staff I would have had a better chance.

Since Claire and I did most of the work I couldn't believe we wouldn't end up on top our senior year, myself as editor and Claire as feature page. I figured they would toss the gossip column to Joan since she was so good at gossip and knew absolutely everything about everyone's love life.

Joan's boyfriend was 17 so he wasn't yet eligible for the draft. He was smart in school and wanted to go to college instead of the Army but Joan didn't think he'd be able to avoid the draft. Boys were being drafted left and right, some on their 18th birthdays.

I worked very hard that junior year. I wanted to get a scholarship to Northwestern University and get into journalism school. Fiction was something to play around with in my spare time. I wanted to be a war correspondent and work for TIME or LIFE or a big newspaper. That's why any experience in reporting was so important to me. I volunteered for any writing job on the paper and Joan's boyfriend became a friend of mine since I helped him whenever I could. I was careful not to get too friendly, though I secretly thought I was better looking than Joan.

The summer before my junior year my family rented a cottage in Michigan City, Indiana. They rented cottages every summer at resort towns around Lake Michigan, I was sure, to keep me from going to summer camp. The idea of getting away on my own for a whole summer was too beautiful for me to even contemplate. I knew it would never happen. And I was right. My mother insisted I was too prone to illness to be gone all summer. Heaven knows what I would pick up in the woods. I guess she was right but I wanted to go anyway.

This particular summer I met a girl who went to the high school across the street from mine. The schools were in different districts but so close the students knew each other well. Liz was the daughter of friends of my parents, so she was automatically okay for me to associate with. We got along pretty well. She had a steady boyfriend, who she talked about all the time, and we went to the beach or to movies together that summer in Michigan City, meeting girls and boys from all over the state. I had more fun than I ever thought I would.

Liz belonged to a sorority at her school and wanted to know if I would like to join. I would be the only member from my school, which appealed to me. I needed to broaden my horizons, get some experience in how to handle different situations. She was the incoming president and planned to invite me to their first meeting in the fall to see how I liked the girls and how they liked me.

I went to the meeting and was accepted. I guess I wasn't a threat to their boyfriends, the main criteria. I must say I looked the best I had since I was a baby in the North Woods and what boys there were gathered around Liz and me at the beach all summer. I think she told her sorority sisters I would be an asset. Being attractive to boys was the main asset those days.

The meetings were interesting, the doings at the other school even more social than at my school. The talk was about boys, boys, boys, even though the boys were almost gone. I listened as hard as I could, trying to pick up the nuances of dating and being a girlfriend, something I wasn't even sure I wanted to be. My friend Sam from the park had gone off to the Army and it was like he had never existed. I guess he wasn't as important to me as I had thought.

The invisible plastic wrap I had felt at school that first day wrapped itself around me even more tightly as I realized how different I was from the sorority girls. Our interests were on other planets. Books were never mentioned. We liked the same music but I was getting more interested in classical music by then, which was out of their orbit.

They fixed me up with dates and I went, terrified I would not know how to act. I had been on dates before but this was different. This was the Real Thing, with men home on leave from the Army or Navy. I was able to avoid my parents' eagle eye because I slept over at Liz's house and the dates picked us up there. Liz dated friends of her fiancé, who had gone into the Army. He had given his okay.

It was fun, I guess. We went to clubs where they played jazz and the men all drank. Since they were in the service, they were served, no questions asked. I never said much. I was trying so hard to watch how everyone acted I was stiff as a board. When my date asked me a question, I answered yes or no. I must have made a great impression.

But when he took me back to Liz's, pecked my cheek and said goodnight, I was so relieved to finally be out of the situation, I thought there was something wrong with me. It was okay to have wild crushes on perfect strangers but when I had to go out with a possible crush, that was something else.

My social life staggered along the rest of my junior year, my attention fixed on the prize, the editorship. The year was winding down and Joan was getting more certain that she would win out over everyone. I was nervous, figuring she must know more about it than we did.

The last week of school arrived. The staff gathered in the newsroom, the journalism classroom, to hear the news. Joan was hanging onto my arm, unable to conceal a big grin. I couldn't understand her. She knew nothing about how to put a paper together. I didn't know a lot but I had been watching and helping with the layouts and proofreading and I had some idea. Her boyfriend wouldn't even be there to help her. He had just gotten his draft notice, on his 18th birthday. He had told me this while we were working on the final issue, the front page left open for the news about the staff.

The journalism teacher sat at the back of the room smiling encouragingly, her usual expression. I couldn't tell anything from her. Then the editor got up and made the announcements.

"For editor-in-chief, in appreciation of all the work and dedication she has put into the paper since she started, we name Claire. As feature page editor, Joan will handle the job admirably. And as the gossip columnist, which you know remains secret until the end of the year, Elaine. Thanks to all of you and have a great year."

I sat there, turned to stone. Me. The gossip columnist, the thing I hated most about the paper and the school. Joan hugged me and hoped I would help her with her new job. Fat chance. My days of helping anyone were over. I congratulated Claire, shook the editor's hand, disentangled myself from Joan and left the room and the school to catch my bus. On the way out the door I met Esther, her face bright, expectant. I had told her about my hopes, unable to keep them completely to myself. She was the only person who knew how much I wanted that editor's job.

"Well?" she said.

"Ask Joan," I muttered, and pushed past her.

On the way home I worked hard to keep my tears hidden. My heart was beating so fast I thought I was going to die on the bus. It was lucky there was no one home but my grandmother because the anger was boiling and raring to get loose at anyone who came near. I went into my sleeping porch and started raging. How could this have happened? After all I had done, after how hard I had worked, my dedication. The newspaper business was going to be my life's work and I couldn't even make it to editor! Well, they would be sorry. The whole school would be sorry. After I finished with them in the gossip column there might even be a riot.

At dinner I didn't say anything. Nobody would know. I planned to keep this disgusting secret from my family so at least some people might have a good opinion of me. I had not realized until then how much I valued their good opinion.

That night not even Dave Garroway could console me. I listened and the tears finally came about midnight, making my pillow wet and keeping me up even longer. What would I do? How could I keep my head up next term when everyone knew I was not the editor? Well, I was going to tough it out, work on the paper every day as I always had, and tell no one how I really felt. No one cared anyway. I sobbed, and vowed this was not the end of my ambitions. So I wouldn't be a war correspondent. So I wouldn't work on newspapers. There were the magazines, local news sheets, books I hadn't even thought about writing until that moment. And before that, Northwestern where I had won an honorary scholarship to the journalism school, meaning no money but I was in.

I knew more opportunities were waiting there. Plotting my future without the editorship, I finally fell asleep.

CHAPTER 12

ROMANCE

The summer before my senior year we went off to another resort town on Lake Michigan and luckily Liz's family went with us. Liz didn't have a clue about the trauma I had just suffered and it was hard for me to tell her. She and her friends, my sorority sisters, had no idea of any other ambition after high school or college but a husband, married life and eventually, a family.

She was going to think I was crazy, wanting to work and not be supported. It wasn't being supported that bothered me. It was that I still had no idea how to form a relationship with a man. I had been trying since my freshman year to figure out the components of this kind of a relationship without success. I didn't like the boys who liked me and the ones I thought I might like had girlfriends, lots of girlfriends.

At the beach that summer Liz and I talked about our futures. Hers was set. She was going to marry the boy she had been dating for four years. She had just graduated. This was her last summer of vacation with her folks.

"I start college in the fall – I'm not sure about leaving home. Even though I'm only going downstate, to Illinois. It's scary. Even scarier is thinking about my wedding."

"Why scarier?" I asked, surprised that someone else was afraid of the future.

"Oh, I don't know. Getting married. Even though I know Albert so well. It's just – scary."

She paused a minute. "The wedding isn't until after Albert comes back from the war."

Another pause. Maybe she was thinking, "if" he comes back from the war.

I told her about my ambitions, how I wanted to be a writer, how I wasn't sure where I would fit in, but I was going to find out as soon as I could.

To my surprise, she said, "That's wonderful! I envy you for having such big plans." She sighed. "My life in comparison sounds so dull."

She told me about how it felt to be in love and couldn't imagine that I had never even been a little in love. I didn't think my wild crushes qualified so I kept them quiet. The way she felt about things wasn't anything like the way I felt about the same things, so I listened and didn't add much to the conversation. Luckily she was a great talker. She talked about her family, how she was going to miss them, how she had hated to leave high school, how now she had to grow up and have responsibilities.

It had never occurred to me that when I graduated I would have responsibilities. I only thought about a career at some place where I would be able to write and be involved in publishing. As for leaving my family and high school, I couldn't wait.

She asked me questions to get me talking, and I tried to answer them. Like about how I felt when I went out with a boy, when he kissed me, all that. It made me uncomfortable to talk about it. I changed the subject whenever I could.

Everything in our lives was governed by the war. We had rationing and couldn't get nylon stockings and had to wear thick silk stockings that bunched at the ankles. We had a lot of gripes but kept them between ourselves because of the war effort. That summer at the beach things were quiet. It was 1942, the war was raging and the

Germans were overrunning all of Europe. I tried to keep my fears in check. I tried not to think, what if the Germans beat us? Liz was afraid too since her boyfriend was in the European theatre and in the middle of things. She let me read some of his letters and that didn't encourage me much. So far as I knew no one I was related to or acquainted with had been killed but the war was just heating up.

There was a local USO and we persuaded our parents to let us go, to dance with the soldiers. I told my father it was the least I could do for the war effort, on the weekends when he came out to be with us. My mother agreed. My brother, who ran around with the wrong crowd, according to my mother, also agreed, not that his opinion mattered much. My grandmother, who loved it at our cottage because it had a big front porch where she could watch everything on the beach from her rocking chair, did not agree, but she was having too good a time watching everyone to put up major objections. My father only let me go to the USO when he was at the cottage, guarding everything.

After my father finally gave the okay, Liz and I dressed up in our good dresses and high heels and eagerly headed for the USO. The soldiers came from all over the country to an army base near the resort town and crowded into the USO on Saturday night to drink punch and eat sweets and hang around with the local girls. My father was afraid they would get fresh but they really didn't. A lot of them didn't even want to dance.

As we sat at a table waiting to be asked to dance, music was blaring from a jukebox, Benny Goodman, Harry James, Glenn Miller, all of the great dance bands.

A couple of soldiers sat down at the table. One said, "If it's okay with you, we just want to sit and talk. It's the last time we'll be with girls from home before we ship out." It was so sad. They were homesick before they even left.

I guess it was about then I developed a real hatred for war and what it did to the people who had to fight it and the people who waited, some in vain, for the soldiers to come home. All the rah-rah patriotism, the heroics of going into battle, the propaganda to make boys enlist voluntarily, for glory--they didn't mention death--scared me and made me a little sick. I knew we were fighting for our lives and our way of life and we had been left no choice but to pitch in and do our best, but I hated the means, I hated that there were such bad things going on in the world and such bad people threatening us. I didn't know about the death camps yet.

My invisible plastic wrap had protected me from life and how to live it, but it wasn't protecting me from the war. It only made me more frightened because I didn't know how to handle the constant bad news over the radio and in the newspapers. Liz said she couldn't listen. But I couldn't stop listening.

We finally danced with the soldiers.

"Come on," I said, "a little jitterbugging will cheer you up."

And it did. Liz and I with our partners drew a crowd as we twirled and the soldiers threw us under and over and all around. It was great fun, and when the set was finished, they were laughing as we went back to our table and some cokes.

They thanked us and said, "We'll remember this night when we're over there fighting. The two beautiful girls who made us see what we were fighting for."

That night when my father picked us up at the USO, Liz and I felt as though we had really contributed something to the war effort.

Summer was finally over and I had to go back and face my senior year, something I looked forward to only because it was my last year of torture. Things were pretty much the same with Claire in control of the paper. She managed everything with a quiet efficiency and not much imagination but the paper came out on time and the journalism teacher was pleased.

Joan was something else. She did not know what she was doing. The first feature page was a mess. She asked me to help but I said I was too busy digging up gossip for my column. I felt she could have put in a good word for me with her boyfriend-editor. I would have done it for her.

I was getting a kind of perverse pleasure out of reporting the pairings and fallings out of my classmates, most of whom I wouldn't even talk to except to say hello and goodbye. I did pitch in and help Claire, writing stories about school doings and helping with the layout and proofreading.

Every time a paper came out some boy or girl walked into the newspaper office outraged at what the gossip column had said and demanding to know who had written it. Some accused me and I just shrugged and said that it wasn't me, couldn't they see I was involved in the putting together of it all?

Then one day a soldier came into the office, a former editor I had heard about briefly, who had graduated a couple of years before. He had just been drafted into the army and had come back to say goodbye to the journalism teacher and hang out a while. He was leaving in a couple of days.

He was medium height, black curly hair, crinkly, smiling eyes and a crooked grin. He looked like John Garfield, a popular film star. And he looked like a perfect candidate for a wild crush. There he was shaking my hand and smiling at me in a special kind of way and I was going to faint any minute.

"Hi," I said.

"Boy, they didn't have anybody like you on the paper when I worked here."

"Lucky you."

"Well, I wouldn't say that. Until now."

He seemed to pay a lot of attention to me, and I tried to be as nice and sweet as I could, but since being nice and sweet was not my usual style, some small sarcasms did creep in. He seemed to like that and asked if I could go out for a soda after school since his time was very short. I agreed.

When he left, Joan came up to me, and I said, "A wild crush has just walked into my life."

His name was Pete Weiss and he met me in the hall outside the office after the last bell. He said he had spent most of the time talking to the journalism teacher who was a good friend and he had asked her to write to him. Would I write to him? He would be sure to answer me. I said yes as we walked across the street to the little lunchroom for a soda. Out of the corner of my eye I saw Joan talking excitedly to Esther and pointing in our direction. Was I going to be a candidate for my own column?

Pete kidded around a lot, but I could detect his uncertainty about the future. I wanted to tell him I could imagine how he felt, how I hoped he would keep safe and come back so we could continue with our friendship but I couldn't say any of that. Maybe I could write it in a letter.

I said, "I'll be graduating this year and then I start Northwestern in the fall. I can give you my home address and then when I get to school I'll give you that address." Thinking, if we're still writing to each other.

"Northwestern," he said in his rough-cut voice, raising an eyebrow.

I had to stay upright in my chair. I could not pass out. "Yes," I said in a small voice, the best I could muster, "I'm going into journalism school."

He looked at me for a minute. "You want to be a writer?"

I nodded, my voice finally failing me.

"That's what I want to be," he said and we sat there, eyes locked for a long time, not saying anything. He pulled out a paper and a pencil and said, "What's your address? And your telephone number. I'll call you before I leave."

I gave him the information, hoping my knees would hold me up when I got out of my chair. We shook hands. He had to leave. I had to catch my bus, and we went out the door with Pete holding tightly to my arm like he was going to sink.

"I'll call you tonight," he rasped and blew me a kiss as he ran across the street to catch a bus in the other direction.

I moved slowly to my bus stop, hoping the telephone would be unmonitored that night. Hoping he meant what he said and would call. My knees shaking, I got on the bus and wondered if I had dreamed the whole thing. Encounters like that didn't happen too often to me.

In fact they never happened in real life.

If he tried to call that night, I didn't know it. My mother was on the phone with one of her friends until after I went to bed.

Pete and I started a conversation-by-mail that lasted into my freshman year of college. I obsessed over his letters, trying to read as much into what he was saying as I could, and there was plenty of room for interpretation. A very good writer, he knew how to express himself, how to tell how he felt in writing, while I couldn't even express my feelings to myself. His letters made me feel good and bad, good because he wanted a picture of me, he wanted me to write every day. He seemed to need a lot of attention. Bad because I wasn't sure I knew how to handle the situation. Esther and Joan said to go with my heart, which sounded corny to me. Besides, I had no idea what it meant.

Whenever I received an intensely felt letter, I couldn't answer for a while and then he shot back an angry letter. This went on through most of my senior year.

(I wish now that I had kept those letters. They are the places where memory and imagination have failed me.)

When the letters started coming, I could see my grandmother was consumed with curiosity about who they were from, what they said, what they meant. Since my mother was rarely home when the mail came, I was designated letterbox opener, and I took the key after school and sorted the mail in the hall. But my grandmother - they could have used her in the FBI she was so good at snooping. She met me at the front door.

"So, Elaine. Let me see the mail. All for you? So, who's sending you so many letters? Have you got a boyfriend? Does your mama know? Looks like army letters. So who is it?"

I guess she thought she was being subtle, but her command of the language was limited, her mother tongue Russian, and she mostly spoke Yiddish. She came across as subtle as a falling boulder.

I didn't know what she thought could happen. She was able to read enough to tell that the letters came from other states.

I told her, "They're from a friend on the school paper who was drafted and in basic training. He's very homesick so he writes a lot of letters." That seemed to satisfy her until she saw me carrying in the next batch and it started all over again.

About then I decided, in order to be more athletic, more attractive to Pete and other boys, I should learn how to swim. I had gotten doctors' excuses through high school since my mother was sure I would die of pneumonia if I took swimming in gym. I was the only person I knew who couldn't swim. I nagged and nagged and finally she let me enroll in swimming class. It happened to be winter at the time. All the girls wore regulation swimsuits which when wet showed more than they concealed. We were sure the boys' gym classes spied on our swimming class. But we splashed around so energetically we figured they couldn't see too much. After class I walked around the drafty halls with damp hair and clogged ears.

Sure enough, about two weeks after I started the three-times-a-week classes I came down with a sore throat and a fever and was ordered to bed. I had a terrible cough and the doctor diagnosed viral pneumonia. I hated to admit my mother was right again. This time it was really bad because graduation was coming up and I was determined to be there and finalize my liberation from high school. Not only that, there was the prom and I didn't have a date.

My mother did whatever I wanted to keep me from having tantrums that made me cough violently, which I did every hour or so. Her social life was disrupted. She was afraid to go out to lunch for fear I would get out of bed and go back to school. As if I could. The fever kept me so weak and the coughing was so intense, I could barely sit up. I sent her to the library every day with a list of books. I devoured them and she took them back the next day and brought home a new batch. She went to the high school and picked up homework for me which I did in about fifteen minutes so I could continue reading.

I never did learn to swim.

Then a friend of mine called, a boy who worked on the paper from time to time and was a nice smart kid. We had good conversations about things we liked and didn't like. He asked me if I would be well in time for the prom and I said yes, determined to make it so. He asked if I would like to go with him and I said yes.

I would rather have gone with Pete, who was about to go overseas, according to his letters, about to go to war. I worried about him as I lay trapped in my bed, thinking he would get wounded or worse.

I managed to get better, not well, in time for the prom and off we went, my father greeting my date nicely and not asking the usual questions. After all, it was the prom, his daughter was being escorted, actually well enough, and he wasn't going to mess it up. My mother kept her eagle eye on my father through the whole departure, making sure he didn't scare my date. We went off with another couple, the girl's parents driving us, and had a pretty good time, considering my date didn't know how to dance.

I had to get home early because of my precarious health, and by the time the prom was over I was tired and ready to go back to bed. Mission accomplished. Next stop graduation, which was in a couple of weeks. I was determined to be well by then and put myself on a regimen of food and rest that my mother couldn't contradict, since it was what she would have told me to do if she had had the chance. She was happy not to have to go to the library every day, and concentrated on the trouble my brother kept getting into. He had just gotten kicked out of school again and my parents were shopping for a special school for him.

A few weeks before the prom, the last issue of the newspaper had come out, revealing the name of the gossip columnist. Me. I had written the column from my bed and had paired everyone up with the wrong people. I don't even want to think about what would have happened if I had been at school. Joan called me and told me all about it. I was so sick I could barely make it to the phone from the sleeping porch. The outcry was tremendous, she said, and she had to take the brunt of it since the column was on her page and everyone knew I was home sick and blamed her for writing it.

I think that was what made me recover so quickly. I laughed so hard at the mischief I had caused. I was smiling for days. By the time I came back to school it was almost forgotten and except for some ferocious looks from some boys and snubs by some girls, everything kept moving along to graduation.

I wrote Pete about the fallout from the column. He wrote back, saying he hadn't laughed so much since he went into the army. It cheered him up before shipping out. I was glad the column was good for something.

Graduation day. We were all in line in our caps and gowns waiting to march in to the strains of "Pomp and Circumstance." Luckily I was able to march in with my friends Joan and Esther, since the line was not arranged alphabetically. They were both crying. A lot of the other girls were crying too, their mascara running down their cheeks. I was probably the only girl who could have cried with no aftereffects, because I didn't wear mascara. But crying was not for me. I was ready to run full speed down that aisle, grab my diploma and get out of there forever. Graduation day was one of the happiest days of my life.

CHAPTER 13

UNIVERSITY

Many years later, I looked back at what my Northwestern education must have cost my father. Northwestern was expensive even then and I insisted I had to live on campus to get the full benefit of the experience, which was even more costly. He made a decent amount of money as a lawyer for the city of Chicago, and we lived in that apartment which didn't seem to require a lot of rent. My aunt and uncles had moved out long ago and except for my mother's extravagances - a mink coat, expensive jewelry - which my father bought happily, who knows what he went without? - and my brother's tuition at the special school he didn't bother to attend very often, we seemed to be able to make ends meet.

My tuition was another matter. I still don't know how my father managed it for four years, together with room, board, books and supplies and the wardrobe I put together. It didn't occur to me to worry about where the money was coming from. Since early childhood I had been kept from knowing about any inner family crises or conflicts. I knew nothing about anything.

I had long ago given up trying to find out from my family how life was lived, and just went along taking whatever I wanted, my father giving it all without hesitation. My mother went along too, and she knew about our finances. Maybe they felt I was their only hope for happiness or sense of accomplishment, or success, in the eyes of their friends, since my brother was obviously not going to give them anything. But then, he had never gotten anything. No love, no understanding, no attention.

My demands did not assuage the hole inside me, the empty place where feelings and emotions were supposed to be. I was hoping that living in the new environment of Northwestern, exposed to different people and experiences, would fill it finally and then maybe I could become a real person who felt and acted like other girls my age.

And then there was Pete. I assumed he was on a ship that was taking him somewhere to fight the war, and I would get a letter when he arrived. Nothing much happened that summer except my excitement grew at the prospect of college. Esther had gotten into Northwestern too but she was not in Journalism, she was in Liberal Arts and was going to live at home and commute. Joan was going to the University of Wisconsin to be with her boyfriend, who had gotten out of the Army draft.

My dorm was an old building on campus for the overflow freshman registration. Usually all female freshmen lived at Willard Hall, which was in the Quads and the best place to be. I was so happy to be living anywhere but home, I didn't even care. I decided to go through rush week and get into a sorority. And then I would be in the Quads too.

I knew I wasn't sorority material. I was not too friendly and I rarely smiled. But since I knew all this, and my wardrobe measured up, I figured it would be easy to cover it up at the teas and parties. I didn't count on being bored out of my skull with the stupid conversations. "Where did you go to high school?" "What's your major?" over and over. The girls seemed nice but my social skills were not keen enough for the constant smiling and dressing up and making small talk hour after hour. I passed the first round and was invited back to one of the sororities but lucky for me I didn't get in. I wouldn't have known how to refuse and would have been even more miserable than I already was.

Miserable because my roommate from Pennsylvania was a person I hated on sight. Her brother, a fraternity boy, she assured me, promised to get her into the best sorority since she was a "legacy." She bragged about it non-stop. She bragged about everything non-stop, her grades, her brother, her boyfriend, her family. She was asked to join the same sorority that invited me back. Can you imagine us both in the same house for four years? I would have either shot her or myself.

Living was very tense for a while until I met a girl who would be my friend for life. She was from Chicago and had worked in her family's business before enrolling at Northwestern in Speech school. She was a little older and as friendly and nice as my roommate was the opposite. My roommate and I lived together but didn't speak. It was the best for both of us. When she was accepted by the sorority in the second quarter, she moved out and I moved in with my friend May and never saw that roommate again. It was like the wicked witch had been carried off by a dragon, or an evil spell. Maybe I had wished it.

School finally began and I was swallowed up in the rounds of classes and other activities. I went to class with much confidence, school never having been a problem for me. In Freshman English we had to write a lot of papers and study grammar, not my favorite thing. I did my best and I got a C on the mid-term. I couldn't believe it. I had never gotten a C in my life! And in English! And I was supposed to be a writer! I could see Northwestern was going to require more effort than high school. I really worked hard and got a B plus the next test and felt a little better.

I loved walking around the campus that first month, watching the students hurrying to their classes, some carrying their things in bags and satchels. I delighted in being one of them, in a skirt and sweater like the other girls, arms loaded with books and note pads.

I listened closely in my classes and took many notes. I seemed to sit near the same people since we were all freshmen and were seated alphabetically. In the lecture courses, like political science, we sat in large auditoriums, wherever we could find a seat.

The freshman dorm was quaint, a building made of wood, not like the stone structures on campus. I had a brief recall of my fear of fire when I was small but quickly forgot it in the rush of new acquaintances. Outside of my first roommate, the girls were very good looking and friendly, seeming to know everything about boys and dating, whispering and giggling in their rooms, not about their classes, I'm sure. They came from all over the country, Kansas, Oklahoma, Texas, a couple even from California.

I admired them, so tall and shapely with gorgeous men resplendent in their uniforms, either local ROTC or servicemen on leave, picking them up for dates. They came home right at curfew, lipstick smeared, clothes disarranged, sometimes smelling of alcohol, shoes untied, messy, but glowing. I wanted desperately to know what they had been doing. I didn't even dare to guess. My education, I felt, was about to take a great leap forward.

The letters from Pete began again. He wrote about the fighting. He couldn't say where he was, but it was awful by the sound of it. He wrote about his buddies, what happened to them, and what happened to him. The writing was different, not so internal. He was having a major life experience and it was changing him.

I wanted desperately to be in the middle of a major life experience too, but on campus things just moved deliberately, in manufactured calm. I was afraid to approach my housemates with personal questions. They treated me like their little sister and looked with curiosity at the letters from Pete on the mail table in the hall. They asked if the letters were from my boyfriend in the service and I smiled and said yes. One small point for me.

Christmas break came almost too soon and I had to go home for two weeks. I packed my things and waited for my mother to pick me up and take me back to That Place. I didn't know how it would feel. I knew it wouldn't be pleasant. It was never pleasant.

My mother hit me with questions on the ride home. What was school like, were the girls nice, did I like my classes, who had I met and on and on. I answered in monosyllables, saying I would be very busy while I was home. I had books to read, papers to write, no time to spend on socializing.

She was a little subdued at that and spent the rest of the ride talking about how my brother was such a problem, he had met a girl at his special school and was carrying on with her, my mother's term for romance. My brother was about eleven.

Finally we were at the apartment and I was bombarded by all the old feelings -- oppression, depression, dismay. I vowed I would not be pushed down by anything. I was going to read, write, pass the time productively and then, happy day! get back to school.

Some boys, not in the army yet or rejected for service, called and we went out. I was bored. I would rather have been home reading a good book, or at school, hanging out with my dorm mates, hearing about their escapades. I was not quite one of them, but I was a good audience. I was always ready to listen. And they liked me. But they never talked about what I needed to know.

While I was home we had a family gathering and I saw my aunts and uncles and cousins on my father's side. Del and I had a great time talking about school. She went to the University of Illinois at Champagne, and had met a soldier from Rantoul, an air force base near her school.

She whispered to me, "We're serious. I don't know how to tell my parents that we might get engaged. He's from Oklahoma. My mother will have a fit. You know what I mean."

I spent New Year's Eve at home with my grandmother listening to the festivities on the radio. Things were subdued because of the war and Times Square was filled with servicemen, the announcer said. Everyone hoped the war would be over soon, although the way it was going, I thought that was wishful thinking. My parents had gone off to a party with their friends, calling out, "Happy New Year!" before they left. It would be happy as soon as I was back in school. No one knew where my brother was. No one mentioned him. It was as if he didn't exist.

Finally the vacation was over and I was brought back. I was never so happy to see a place in my life. I walked into the front hall and on the mail table were piles of letters from Pete. My dorm mates kidded me and said it looked like someone was missing me. I smiled, speechless. I had never been the center of attention because of a boy. I gathered up the letters, almost emptying the table, and ran to my room to read them in private. I sorted them by postmark and settled down happily, really glad to hear from him. I hadn't written to him the whole time I was home.

I was overwhelmed by the outpouring of emotion in Pete's letters. Some were short, only one line asking why I didn't write. Some were long accounts of battles fought, friends killed, near misses for him. He was a foot soldier, a grunt, as he called himself, fighting the war in the trenches, often outnumbered, usually cold and wet and hungry. It sounded like a war novel by Hemingway.

But most of the letters were about how he felt, how much he missed me, how he couldn't wait to see me again. The war was turning, things were looking up. Maybe it would be over soon and he would come home. The thought threw me into a fit of terror. I was still the little freshman college student, wondering if I had any emotions at all. He was a man, a soldier. A stranger.

I wrote him many letters after that, trying to fill the space in his life that he had allotted me, being compassionate and caring. I dredged up the meager writing skills I had developed so far, and he bombarded me with letters of hope for a wonderful future. Future! I was still working on getting rid of my past.

School activities overwhelmed me and I was pressed to read and write and talk my way through my sophomore year. My friend May had left to get married and I had a new roommate. Her name was Gina. She was in Speech.

We had to move out of our freshman digs and ended up in a small hotel converted into a dorm and it was great. We had a corner room with two big windows and a private bathroom. A lot better than the crowded sorority houses on campus. That was the only trouble. We had to walk about six blocks every day to get to class or the library where I spent a lot of time. In winter the wind blowing off Lake Michigan a couple of blocks away was brutal.

I had a warm coat and the walk was bracing and I had so much to look forward to in my classes that I didn't mind. I had met a bunch of girls at the dorm and we were a pack, a crowd. I was finally a part of something I had always wanted. A lot of friends. Life was heady. My grades were good, my social life limped along but there were the letters from Pete. Words were always easier for me to deal with than actual people. I could say I was finally happy for the first time in years.

Then my Uncle Phil was killed in the war and I had to go home for the funeral. It was very sad and, in 1944, we were beginning to see a glimmer of the end of the war so it was especially tragic. I wrote Pete about it and his letters back were philosophical, almost fatalistic. He hoped he would make it, he couldn't be sure, no one could, to pray for him and send him luck. I wrote him that I would, although I wasn't much for praying.

Toward the end of 1944 he wrote me that he was coming home. I almost fainted at the thought of actually seeing him, face-to-face. I hadn't ever gotten to know him in person. I had just seen him that one afternoon at high school, it seemed many years ago.

I had big conferences with my friends, with my roommate Gina, who was experienced in these things. I had the feeling she thought I was still a baby, and maybe she was right. If anything was going to come of this meeting with Pete, I would have to grow up, fast.

I did look pretty good, if I say so myself. My hair was dark and long and curled under. I was still short, still thin but filled out where I had to be filled out. Gina said I should smile a lot. I looked real good when I smiled, she said.

"Just be yourself. He'll be so happy to see you he won't care about anything else." She nodded in emphasis.

"But he thinks we have a future together," I wailed. "I don't want to hurt him but that's not what I'm thinking, at least not yet."

"Don't jump ahead of things," Gina advised. "Just play it as you see it, and as you feel it."

"I hope I feel something besides terror."

She just smiled.

The day arrived and so did Pete. At school, waiting in the dorm lobby, in his uniform, with everyone peeking around corners. I walked up to him and he threw his arms around me and kissed me so passionately, that if he hadn't had me in a tight hug, I would have fallen down from shock.

I pulled back finally and said, "Hi." He looked about the same as I remembered him, but there was a grimness about his mouth, and his eyes were hard until he faced me.

We looked at one another for a long time and then he said, taking my arm, "Let's get out of here."

I kept flashing glances at him, trying to get the feel of things as we left the dorm. He looked older, haggard. The happy-go-lucky wisecracking guy I wanted to see again had been taken over by a care-worn grown-up.

And so began a very painful period. He wanted me to commit, I had no idea to what. I asked a lot of questions, as usual, which he thought I should have known the answers to. He knew the answers and didn't think he should have to educate me. He didn't like to talk much about it.

He was gruff and abrupt and scared me. He just wanted to be physical. I couldn't be physical. I didn't know how and I was afraid to try. I was 18 and should have felt something more than fear. I should have felt inklings, tinglings, something.

He came over to the dorm every evening and we would sit on a couch in one of the little alcoves, kissing and murmuring. I tried to go along as best I could but he was not gentle or sweet, not romantic at all, he was impatient and sometimes angry.

"I waited so long for this. I can't understand what's wrong. Why are you hesitating? Why don't you respond?"

I told Gina about it. She said, "It will take some time. He's been through a lot and is probably trying to work through it. He needs help from you."

I said, "How can I help him? I can't even help myself!"

He wanted marriage. I couldn't imagine myself married. Living with him. Afraid of everything. Only doing what he wanted. I flashed back to my early home life and said no, marriage was not for me. I told him I was going to New York after graduation to have a career.

The next night he came over and started in as though nothing had happened, as though marriage was still on the table. He grabbed me and started to kiss me with more ardor than usual. The urgency, the press of his body – I pulled back, weak with fear, I think it was fear, and said, "I can't do this. I can't – I can't be what you want. I don't – I don't think we should see each other again."

I felt like a rat but I couldn't do anything else.

He stared into my face. He saw the fear. I imagined he could smell the fear.

He had built such expectations, made me his dream girl, his fantasy perfect mate. Lana Turner would have had trouble living up to what he expected.

"Tell me why you're so scared. I love you. Why does that scare you? Don't send me away. Please don't."

Tears came. I couldn't answer. I looked at him dumbly and shook my head, trying to get up from the couch.

His shoulders fell. He took my hands and kissed my fingers, gently, sweetly. Where had this Pete been when I wished for him?

He said, "Thank you, little Elainie, for keeping up my spirits during the war. Your letters, your picture gave me hope when there wasn't any, and I'll never forget you for that. Maybe you were too convincing, maybe I read too much into what you said but you see I was in love with you. I'm still in love with you. I'll carry your face and voice with me forever."

He kissed me on the forehead, on both cheeks, and got up and left as I watched through tear-filled eyes.

I felt terrible for a while. I felt I had ruined his life, and then the press of school and the end of the war took over and Pete slowly faded. He had occupied my thoughts for so long, my romantic thoughts formed by his letters and the many novels I had read. The real-life, earthy, human Pete didn't turn out to be the Pete I imagined. Confronting reality, I caved.

Just about then President Roosevelt died. I remember looking out the window of my dorm and thinking the world would be a strange place without him in charge -- a strange and dangerous place. Like the ground was suddenly insubstantial, unable to hold us up.

I was a junior, it was 1945 and GIs were coming home and enrolling in college on the GI Bill. Strange faces began appearing in my journalism classes as the old familiar classmates vanished. We were graded on a curve and the curve had shot upward with experienced men taking their places in class and cutting away the students who had been borderline. I hadn't realized there were so many borderlines.

I was in a whirl of work and dating. Sometimes I had to read three books in one night, no great feat for me from my past habits, and then I went out on one or two dates afterward. I don't even remember who the dates were. Suddenly the campus was crowded with good-looking, smart men and all of us were having a whale of a time. There were so many men it was easy not to commit to one. This was what college was supposed to be, I thought. Not much sleep but plenty of fun and work.

My family receded into dimness, my mother calling from time to time to complain that she never heard from me. I pleaded an overload of work. After all I was a junior now and in my major at Journalism school.

The next two years passed quickly. My roommate Gina and I made plans to go to New York after graduation. She was going to work in the theatre and I was going to get a writing job. I had been dating her brother Brad, who looked like Dana Andrews, a current movie star. Nothing serious, I made sure, but nice to be with. Christmas was especially fun since her family was Italian and they celebrated with great gusto.

Brad was in awe of my father since he had political ambitions. He was a law student, and thought that working as a lawyer at City Hall was the ultimate. I didn't have the heart to tell him about my father's ambitions to be a judge and how he had just been removed from the ticket, again, because Mayor Daley the First had someone else to put on. This disappointment helped send my father into a deeper withdrawal from reality and he was even harder to talk to. But he would always listen to me.

Graduation drew near and I was elected to the Journalism honorary society, so I was in a sorority after all. But this one meant something. My parents didn't have a clue about my post graduation plans. They thought I was going to New York for two weeks as my graduation present.

I had to find a place to stay. I didn't know anyone in New York except a friend of my Aunt Sophie, Miriam Kaplan, whom I had met briefly when she came to visit Sophie and her family. I asked Aunt Sophie for Miriam's address and wrote a letter, asking if I could stay with her until my roommate arrived in New York and we found an apartment.

She wrote back that her place was being painted, she didn't have room, she couldn't have a guest just then, but I answered that I didn't mind being inconvenienced and would be there in a month. She lived in Brooklyn, she obviously didn't want me, but I didn't care. Nothing was going to stop my Great Adventure. I had some money from graduation presents and some savings and I was eager to be off. I had never been really on my own before and had no idea what it involved. It was probably just as well I didn't know.

CHAPTER 14

NEW YORK

A week in advance, unable to wait, I packed my meager wardrobe for the trip to New York on the Pacemaker, an overnight coach train from Chicago. My wardrobe was meager because hemlines had suddenly fallen to the ankles, the New Look, they called it, leaving me with a closetful of very short skirts.

Not wanting to give away my career plans to my mother, I skipped an extended shopping trip and bought a long coat and decided it would have to cover everything. If I packed too many suitcases, she was going to get suspicious. I thought she was suspicious anyway.

She asked, "How could you force yourself on a woman you only met once, a woman who doesn't even want you to stay with her?"

"It'll be all right. I'll be sightseeing all day (meaning job-hunting) and won't even see Miriam much. Besides a hotel is too expensive."

My mother asked, "What are you going to do with the money we gave you for a graduation present if you aren't going to spend it on your trip?"

I mumbled something about necessities, food, entertainment, New York is very expensive. She seemed satisfied, but she wasn't happy about it. She had been frowning for days, the more she saw me smile.

Finally it was time. I was boarding the Pacemaker, clutching my suitcase and my purse, waving out the window at my parents as the train pulled out of the station. I didn't notice my surroundings, I didn't notice it was getting dark, I couldn't remember what station we were leaving from. We were moving and that was what I wanted.

Then it sank in. I was leaving home. Alone. Gina, my roommate, wasn't coming for a month, family business, she said. I was supposed to find us an apartment, a job for me, and generally manage things for myself. I was going to be out in Brooklyn, miles from Manhattan, the Promised Land, and relying on the subway to get me up and back. I had never been on a subway in my life.

The weight of it all hit me like a lightning bolt and I shrank into my seat. To stop full-scale panic, I decided to think of things one at a time and concentrated on how I would get to Miriam's apartment after we pulled into New York the next morning. I decided a cab would be best since I had no idea where Brooklyn was or how to get there.

Daydreaming in my seat, watching the countryside speed past, I rehearsed my meeting with Miriam, practicing how charming and sweet I would be and how she would be happy at my arrival in spite of her objections. The excitement, the soothing movement of the train, the lullaby of clickety-clacking wheels made me sleepy and I put my head back to relax.

The conductor woke me to take my ticket. I jumped, at that moment not knowing where I was, and fumbled in my purse. After he passed, I decided it was time for dinner. My mother had packed a sandwich, some of her tasteless chicken that I had slathered with ketchup, and I began to eat it, as a cart came wheeling down the aisle selling drinks. I bought a Coke, some chips and a cookie, and I enjoyed my dinner, feeling very grown up and thinking things were going well. So far.

After my earlier nap, I found it hard to sleep. The seats went back only a little. From time to time I got up to use the bathroom at the end of the car, nervously leaving my suitcase in the rack above my seat and taking purse, magazines, books, toiletries case -- everything-- with me.

When I returned, I looked into the blackness of the window and waited for the clickety lullaby to put me to sleep. I kept thinking, what kind of job would I get? I had applied by mail to the women's magazines, but they all said I had to start in the steno pool. Everyone started in the steno pool. Since I was a terrible typist, having scorned such menial skills in high school, there was no way I would pass a typing test. Besides, I wasn't going to New York to be a typist. I would get a copy of the New York Times and was sure I would find a job.

As best I could, I tried to ignore the fluttering in my stomach, the uncertainty of what was going to happen, my inability to control events.

My mind ran on and on spinning scenarios about jobs I was going to find, people I would meet, imagining a wonderful life, until I felt the light on my closed eyelids and saw it was morning and we were almost there.

By the time I found a cab to take me to Brooklyn, and arrived at Miriam's apartment building, the morning was almost gone. The constant clamor of traffic, hordes of people pushing their way down New York streets, honking cars and cabs and trucks, traffic jams getting out of Manhattan, had filled me with anxiety. I was supposed to maneuver my way through this? My mother's supercilious smile, saying, You've finally bitten off too much, flashed at me as I paid the cabdriver, and I vowed I would make it. I would be okay.

Standing outside Miriam's door, I held my breath to calm my racing pulse. What if she wasn't home - on purpose? What if she was mean? What if -- then the door opened and there she was with a big smile.

"Elaine! So good to see you again. Come in, come in. My place isn't very big but --"

"Oh, I'm so glad to be here," I blurted in relief. I looked around at the tiny living room, the small alcove in the corner, the mini kitchen. "This is just great! I don't take up much room. You'll see."

"Put your things in there." She pointed to the alcove. "That couch opens into a bed and the small table here has a couple of drawers you can use. I'm afraid we'll have to share the hall closet."

As she spoke she opened the closet and I saw coats and jackets and a small empty place in the corner. The alcove was an ell off the living room, the table hugging a corner wall with two narrow drawers.

Well, it wasn't as though she hadn't warned me. Thank goodness there were no signs of the painters she had mentioned.

"Are you hungry? I've made some sandwiches for lunch." Not waiting for an answer she led me around a corner into a small dining area with a table set for two.

I had dropped my suitcase on the alcove couch and as I followed her I said in a small voice, "May I use the bathroom to clean up?"

"Right this way." She opened a door in the hall and there was the only bathroom in the place. No problem. I was used to one bathroom per family. But this was so small I had to go in sideways to close the door. She handed me a towel and a washcloth.

"What would you like to drink?" she said through the door.

"Just water would be fine." I was suddenly so thirsty I could have drunk an ocean.

She brought tuna salad sandwiches and chips, some cut up watermelon, and large glasses of ice water. It was a welcoming feast. My fears were slipping away and I looked at Miriam, really looked at her, for the first time.

She was a tall broad woman, with reddish hair and glasses, small features but a pursed mouth, like she had seen a few things. I guessed she was early 50's. Aunt Sophie had told me she had never married.

"So what are your plans?" she said.

"I'm planning to get a job as soon as possible and look for an apartment for my college roommate and me. She'll be here within the month. But I can move in before she gets here," I said hastily as she started to speak.

She nodded. "The New York Times is over there on the end table," pointing to the living room. "Might as well get started after lunch."

Nothing like getting the rush act the first minute.

We chatted as we ate. She told me the subway station was on the corner and there was an express into Manhattan every morning at 8 a.m., meaning I'd better be on it.

"I work at a hospital in Brooklyn so I don't have to travel very far. I'm usually home every evening so we can pool our resources and share the dinner chores."

I said that would be fine, wondering what she would want me to do, since at home I had never been allowed in the kitchen to do anything but eat, and at school everything had been done for me. It was time I learned. I was almost 21 years old.

I helped clear up the lunch dishes, and then settled on the couch with the newspaper. I turned to the help wanted pages. It was not Sunday so the listings were rather sparse. But there was one -- a brides book was looking for a bright young writer to work in a small office. I took down the number and called, and spoke to the man on the other end.

"When can you come in for an interview?" he said.

"Tomorrow morning?"

"Fine. Bring a resume of your past experience and your education. Here's the address."

I wrote it down. My creative talents were about to get a workout writing the resume, since I had no work experience at all. I figured he couldn't check whatever I wrote because everything was in Chicago.

I asked Miriam if I could use the typewriter that I saw on a small desk in the corner of her bedroom.

She said I could, grudgingly, and then said she was going to the store to get some dinner for us and would help me with the resume on her return.

I said thanks, not mentioning I didn't need any help, and went to work.

By the time she returned I had manufactured a two-page resume, summer jobs made up, time on the school paper magnified, stories written my whole life, journalism credits, Northwestern degree, journalism honorary, the whole deal. Miriam was impressed.

She told me how to get to my appointment the next day, said to wait until Sunday to look for an apartment, the listings would be better, then went into the kitchen to put things away and fix dinner.

"Do you want any help?"

She said, "Why don't you unpack and get everything ready for tomorrow?"

I crammed what I could into the closet, putting in my long coat first, and then filled the tiny drawers with my underwear. My toiletries kit would come with me into and out of the bathroom since the bathroom was too small to stow anything.

The phone rang.

Miriam said, "It's your mother."

"How is everything? Was your trip uneventful? Are you all right? You don't have a cold, do you?"

I had just left home the day before. Even I couldn't catch a cold that fast. I assured her everything was fine, Miriam was fine, the apartment was fine and I was going sightseeing tomorrow. Miriam looked out of the kitchen when I said that.

So I had to tell her my plans for staying in New York and having a career and that my folks didn't know anything about it.

"Why didn't you tell them?" she asked, apparently thinking any parent would be happy to know this.

I assured her there was no way I could have come if they knew, and if they called I hoped she would keep my secret. She nodded, said yes. I prayed she wasn't going to get on the phone with Aunt Sophie the minute I went to bed.

Next morning I was up early but Miriam was already gone. I had a quick breakfast, dressed in a nicely cut suit even though the skirt was short, and walked to the subway station, feeling very important. I would have this interview, tell him I was going to think it over, and then check again with the big mags, like Mademoiselle, Vogue, Time, Life, etc. Things might be different now that I was actually here. And I had this great resume. I kept saying to myself it was going to be fine, it would work out, stamping on my fears, willing myself to get started on my life.

The office was in a dingy building somewhere in midtown Manhattan, streets piled with garbage bags, people shoving and striding quickly past, seeming not to notice the piled-up trash.

It was September, a warm, sunny day and I entered the dark lobby with mild regret. I guess I should have been nervous, going for my first job interview in New York, but now, with it actually about to happen, I was so full of my own plans, I couldn't be bothered with reality.

The bride's magazine wasn't the one I thought it was. This was a small pamphlet, partially written, to be given away as a premium in department stores, the stores buying them from us. I would be required to finish writing the pamphlet, get it ready for the printer and then go from department store bride's section to department store bride's section, trying to sell it. I kept myself from asking the boss what he was going to be doing while I did all the work. The pay was $35.00 a week.

The boss, the only other person who worked there, was a young overweight, balding man with a big cigar in his mouth. I hated him on sight, the exact kind of person I had avoided all my life. Was I going to work for him? Not if I could help it.

But as it turned out, I couldn't help it. There were no other jobs available to a young inexperienced girl in New York in 1947. Even with an impressive made-up resume and a journalism degree.

The next few days were spent on the phone, calling ads, looking for interviews for other jobs. But I was determined to work in the writing field and the bride's pamphlet was the only thing going. And the boss, let's call him Seymour, was getting impatient. He said he had another girl interested in the job but he thought I was better. When would I make up my mind? I told him Monday because that way, I thought, I could check the Sunday paper. I checked and there was nothing for someone with my non-experience. There were still the typing pools at the magazines, but I knew that was out of the question.

I started work at the bride's book. That is, I started writing it practically from scratch. I asked Seymour who had written the first draft and he said he had but he wasn't satisfied with it. I could see why. He had collected a lot of material, how-to information for brides from various sources, so I had enough to work with, even though I was inexperienced, bride-wise.

I now had a job with a small salary and was living with Miriam who, as the days passed, seemed more eager for me to leave. Not that she said so, but I could tell by the way she looked at me, the way she moved around me in the apartment.

I checked the rentals every day, but I wasn't making enough to rent anything until Gina showed up. Then I heard from her and she was going to arrive in a week! Happy day! Gina wrote that she had a cousin in the Village she was moving in with until we found a place.

It couldn't happen too soon for me. Every day on that subway was a nightmare I tried not to think about. I was squashed in with no way to move my arms, which were pinned to my sides by the crush of people going from Brooklyn to Manhattan every morning. One day I felt fingers moving up my back and trying to get around to my front. I was fearful, angry, frozen in place by the body crush.

I tried to move to see who was behind me or to the side, but I was shorter than almost everyone and I couldn't even move my head. I held my breath and pushed my elbows as far into my sides as I could while lashing out with my foot, first one side then the other. There were some grunts, some ouches but the fingers kept moving. Finally we arrived at the station and I hurried off, not looking to the right or left.

I was delighted when Gina finally arrived in New York and we could look for a place with our combined funds. She was going to direct plays in the New School's Drama department and had a salary as small as mine.

Wonder of wonders, she came up with a sublease in Gramercy Park for three months.

It was a lovely weekend when I moved out of Miriam's apartment, thanking her profusely and promising to keep in touch. Gina and I took over the sublease, complete with our own private key to the park and a wonderful collection of books and records, which we managed to work through in the couple of months we were there. The apartment was dark and dusty, musty and totally New York. Gina's cousin in the Village had had a contact and that was how she had won this prize. Going to work from Gramercy Park was a cinch. I just took a bus and was liberated from the subway. I vowed never to go back to Brooklyn again.

Gramercy Park felt like home. I could spend my life there. I loved going to the park. I loved most that I had a key to get into the park and on weekends could read there with the nannies watching their little kids or wheeling them around the circle. I loved the birds, the flowerbeds, empty now. I loved being in a garden setting in a concrete jungle. For the short while I lived in Gramercy Park, I wasn't afraid.

A giant row developed when my mother found out I had a job and I was not going to come home from my "vacation."

She said, "I won't send you any money, and I'll make sure your father sends you nothing. If you want our help you'll have to beg for it."

"But, Mom –"

"Don't call me until you're ready to come home." I hung up with my ears ringing, relieved that the conversation was over, and a little sad.

"Why is she so impossible?" I said to Gina. We talked about

it and wondered at the vagaries of mothers, deciding they were an iffy project at best.

At work the bride's booklet was nearing completion, Seymour leaning over my shoulder to hurry me along, the stench of his cigar making me gag. Then he invited me up to his place on Long Island for the weekend to fish and relax. Like I was going to relax with him. I talked it over with Gina and she thought the whole thing was a riot and urged me to go.

"You can always stick a chair under your doorknob so he can't get in," she said laughing. Very funny. I needed the job but I wasn't crazy about the perks.

I went reluctantly, thinking, there weren't too many who enjoyed my only defense, sarcastic retorts. Hopefully, a real turn-off. He was doing all the talking as we drove the Long Island Expressway. I had my head out the window like a dog, trying to avoid the smoke from his stogie.

"How come you're so quiet?" he finally said.

"I'm trying not to choke to death from the smoke," I muttered in the nastiest tone I could manage.

Well, what do you know! He threw the cigar out the window. "Sorry. You never said you didn't like my cigar."

I was a little nervous. What was I going to do if he decided to be agreeable? This was a development I hadn't considered.

We stopped on the road for dinner, traffic making progress snail-like, and we chatted about work and the bride's book, which was almost finished. He gave me a short rundown on what my work would be after the booklet was ready.

I was going to ask for a raise when I heard I would be writing to department stores all over the country selling it as well as visiting the local shops. I had been working for him about a month and decided the time wasn't quite right. The place, a restaurant, wasn't right either.

It was a Saturday night and we arrived at his house after dinner, about ten o'clock. I said I was tired and would like to go to bed if he could show me where I was going to sleep. He led me to a damp, moldy-smelling room with a very large bed and said I could stay there. Fortunately there was an attached bath so I wouldn't have to leave the room until morning.

I hated the situation I was in, hated even more the fact that I had been afraid to say no.

Following Gina's instructions, I propped the only chair under the doorknob since there didn't seem to be a lock on the door. Clever of him, I thought, as I imagined him tiptoeing down the hall in the middle of the night.

Sure enough, some time later I awoke to hear the floorboards creaking outside my door and a gentle turning of the knob. Nothing happened and the creaking went back the way it had come.

I took a deep breath but couldn't go back to sleep.

Next morning I came into the kitchen where Seymour was cooking breakfast, puffing away at his cigar. He made pancakes and bacon and we chatted cheerfully, at least I did. He seemed somewhat surly. Then he said we'd have to cancel the fishing because he had to get back to town that afternoon. What a shame, I said, trying not to smile. He never asked me to go to his place for the weekend again.

CHAPTER 15

MOVING AROUND

Gina wanted to know all about my adventure. What I didn't tell her was that I had been terrified the whole time. Seymour was a big man, used to doing what he wanted and I was small and not too strong and had, of my own free will, put myself in a bad spot. Fortunately, things turned out all right but I decided I had been lucky this time.

Then Gina told me the person who owned the apartment we were subletting had called and said she was coming back early, in two days, and asked if we could move out.

I stammered, "What-what are we going to do?"

Gina said, "I worked on it while you were away Saturday. My cousin buys clothes at this boutique in the Village and the owner has a room she wants to rent to two reliable tenants. I went over to see her and the place is very cute. Around the corner from West 4th street, right in the center of things. She said we could move in whenever we wanted so I thought we'd better get started packing."

We gathered up all our belongings and splurged for a taxi to take us to our new place. I almost cried when we left that dark and musty wonderful apartment with the enchanted park attached. But we were headed for Greenwich Village and a new adventure so I tried to perk up and look ahead.

"You'll see," Gina said, "you're going to love it."

It was late afternoon when we arrived at the apartment. Sadie, the woman who owned it, greeted us. She was under five feet and weighed about 150 pounds, round as a bowling ball with stringy blonde hair hanging around her face, piles of beads hanging around her neck, a cigarette dangling from her mouth.

She had an unfamiliar accent as she ushered us into the apartment, which consisted of two rooms, one for her, one for us, a small kitchen and a bathroom we would share with her. The bathroom was big with a floor-to-ceiling window that looked out on a fire escape. High ceilings made the rooms seem extra-spacious.

Our room was large and bright, with the same sunlit window as the bathroom. There were two couches that made up into beds, covered with wildly colored tie-dyed throws, a table and a lamp with fringed shade, assorted ash trays scattered over the table's surface and two easy chairs filled with throw pillows, also tie-dyed, a closet and a dresser we would share. There were a couple of surreal prints on the walls.

It was 1947, too early for the hippie movement but this was the Village and now I knew what "avant garde" meant. The decor was great. Our landlady was part of the decor.

"You are so good at finding us places," I said to Gina. "What would I do without --?"

She gave me a look that made me stop in mid-sentence.

"I wasn't sure how to tell you this," she said. "But I've been accepted at Yale Drama School to study for a masters degree. I have to leave in January."

It was the beginning of November. I had two months before I would be totally alone. I missed Gina already. I had to start thinking about finding another place before I was even used to this one, which I didn't want to leave.

My mother had been calling, trying to be friendly, and the last time she said she and my father were planning a trip to New York over the New Year holidays to see me and go to some plays with me. Would I like that? I said, Sure, I loved the theatre and there were great things on Broadway just then.

The thought of seeing them again, my mother's disapproving glances, my father's vagueness, filled me with feelings I couldn't name. The only bright spot was going to be the horrified look on my mother's face when she walked into our new place. Sadie's Den, we called it.

I tried not to think of Gina leaving. I couldn't afford the rent at Sadie's alone. Where would I go? I forced myself not to panic. I would ask Seymour for a raise. I'd try to find something. But I was not going to think about it until I had to.

Then one day I received a call from Uncle George. He was in town for a couple of days and wanted to take me out to dinner. He said he had a surprise for me. I was so happy to hear from him. I was feeling particularly low just then. Seymour had turned down my request for a raise, even though the bride's booklet was doing very well and he seemed extremely pleased. He said he just couldn't afford to pay me any more. I didn't believe him at all.

Then there was my impending move to somewhere I didn't know, my being alone in what I was beginning to feel was a hostile environment, Gina my only friend who was so busy with her director's job, so social with her colleagues, I hardly saw her.

I told Uncle George I would love to have dinner with him. He suggested that evening. I was overwhelmed to actually hear from someone I cared about and who cared about me to the point that I didn't pay attention to all he was telling me. I did hear him say to meet him at the Russian Tea Room at 6:30 that evening.

"You know where it is," he said. "Right next to Carnegie Hall."

"Yes," I said. I knew where it was.

The Russian Tea Room, one of the poshest places in town. What would I wear? All I had was the long coat that was getting tacky from wearing it every day. I rifled through the closet, pulling out a light blue suit with a skirt that covered my knees. Better if it had been black, but I didn't own anything black.

I walked into the Russian Tea Room, bowled over by the opulence, the elegant crowd, the smells of wonderful food being served. It was brightly colored, reds and yellows mixed with black; ornate samovars on damask covered tables, old Russian in style. I almost expected the Tsar to greet me. But instead, it was the maitre de with a snooty expression. I asked for my uncle's table and he bowed and motioned me to follow him.

Uncle George jumped up and hugged me. I was so happy to see a familiar friendly face, I thought I might cry. Then he turned and I saw someone else at the table. A young girl. He introduced her as Carol, his fiancée. His fiancée! She was younger than I was and I was 21. Uncle George must have been about fifty.

Carol smiled and said, "I'm so happy to meet you. I've heard so much about you from George. You have a lot of spunk, coming to New York alone. I hope we'll be good friends."

She was studying at Juilliard just then so she too was living in New York.

I managed a smile and said I was happy to meet her. And I congratulated her on her engagement to George. How I did all that, I can't imagine. He was marrying a girl so young? And she wanted to do this? She was obviously happy to do this?

Finally I sat down in the chair the waiter was holding and George told me, "Carol was my student for a couple of years, hard years for me. We used to have long confidential talks. I was lonely and she was so sympathetic, caring, endearing."

George was an important person in music, well known in the field, his compositions played by the greats of the violin world. "I felt it was best for Carol, a real talent, to study at Juilliard. She'll be able to advance her studies far past where I could take her." He was speaking softly as Carol looked happily around.

I guess he had seen my shock at the news of his engagement and was trying to convince me of the positive side of things, maybe so I could convince my mother who then could try to convince my grandmother, his mother, who would be hard to convince.

I have no recollection of what I ate that night. I know the waiters brought food and set it down in front of me and then took away the empty plates. George poured wine into my glass to celebrate. As I drank it he kept refilling my glass.

After a while I began to relax. I was probably drunk by then and I started to chat with Carol who was 19 and very excited about the turn her life had taken. She came from a farm in upper Minnesota and her first experience of city life was when her parents had taken her to Chicago to meet George to find out whether he would be willing to teach her.

We laughed and chatted and George seemed pleased that we were getting along so well. I was happy to meet someone who could be my friend in New York when Gina left. I liked Carol although I felt I was more experienced in New York life than she was. I wondered if she was always afraid, as I was always afraid, the fear just below the skin.

The evening ended with an opulent dessert, which George ordered, and we ate it to please him. I didn't know what it was but it was delicious. I was very full and my skirt had gotten tight. I was glad I hadn't taken off my coat. I had forgotten I was wearing it as the dinner progressed.

They insisted on taking me home in a cab since it was late and the weather had turned cold. Carol and I made plans to talk and get together and when they let me off they both hugged me and kissed me and I left the cab feeling much better that I had in a while.

I kept on working and canvassed the department stores with the bride's booklet, as Seymour had instructed. Many of the bridal departments were interested and ordered the book. Seymour complimented me on the good job I was doing but still wouldn't come up with more money.

I thought about threatening to quit, but I had no other job to fall back on, I didn't have time to look, and I had to stay with the best option I had.

Gina was having a great time at her job, she didn't care that she had no money. Besides she was going to Yale on a scholarship. Very soon. She worried that I didn't have a social life and offered to fix me up with one of the actors in her play. I said no thanks, I was fine. I didn't need any more complications in my life.

Then she said she was bringing a friend home for dinner the next day. Could I make my beef stew? I had managed to figure out how to cook a few things by trial and error and recipes I cut out of the paper and the stew was one of the successes. I said sure, I'd be happy to. I would do anything for Gina. It was because of her that I was still sticking to my New York plan. I might have given up and gone back to Chicago long ago without her.

That night I made the stew. I planned to heat it up after work the next day.

When Gina arrived with her guest, I was in awe. He was tall and very good looking, with honey-colored skin and a faint calypso accent. He was one of the actors in her play - they were doing Shaw's "Androcles and the Lion" - and he said he was very hungry and loved beef stew. His name was Eric.

"Should we make Eric sing for his supper?" Gina said with a grin. She was obviously interested in him. I could see why. He radiated sparks but that was nothing compared to the vibes when he stood up near the refrigerator in the kitchen and, as the stew bubbled, sang folk songs in a smoky lilting voice that really knocked me out. He was surrounded by an aura, it was hard to describe, but it warmed me, Gina, the room, everything around us in a sexy, delicious glow.

This one is going to be famous, I thought. With talent like that, he can't miss.

After dinner we sat around and talked politics. He was recruiting for the Communists at the time, very committed, as were most of Gina's friends, but I was not going to go that route. Although my politics were left wing, they were not that far left. Gina hung on every word but did not commit either. It was tough, he was very persuasive and that voice! Like honey-coated heaven.

He left shortly after his harangue, hugging and kissing us both and thanking us for the good dinner. I was a little dazed by the encounter. I had never met a personality like his. Magnetism to the max.

"Are there any others at the school like him?" I asked, seeing why Gina spent so much time there.

"There's nobody like Eric. He's an original. He not only can sing. He can really act. A pleasure to direct. He knows what to do almost before I say anything."

"Sounds like you're falling," I murmured.

She smiled and didn't answer, getting up to help clear the dishes.

Every Sunday morning Sadie would stay in bed, smoke her cigarettes and read the New York Times. Her round fat body, lolling among the scattered newspapers, clad in a transparent red nightgown, cigarette dangling from her mouth, was a sight to behold. I was afraid she would set herself and the apartment on fire, the way the ash hung on the end of that cigarette.

The bed was a mess. Leftovers from her breakfast, filled ashtray, empty cigarette packages, rumpled pillows piled askew, and Sadie, limp strands of hair across her face, wallowing in the center.

My parents were in town for the New Year holiday and they were picking me up to stay with them at their hotel for a week. When I opened the door that Sunday and my mother saw Sadie and her bed, her jaw dropped and she couldn't say a word.

My father hugged me, oblivious to anything but his daughter, and said I looked very well. How were things going? I said fine, and we started to talk about my work as I gathered up my things.

My mother finally said, as I introduced them both to Sadie, "Awfully nice to meet you. Come on, Elaine. We really must be going. We have tickets for a matinee and another show in the evening."

Sadie waved a greeting and smiled but did not move from the bed, settling her folds of fat deeper into the cushions.

And so we left, with me trying not to giggle at the sight of my mother's face. She started in the taxi: how could I live with a person like that? Is this the way she brought me up, to associate with people like Sadie?

"There's nothing wrong with Sadie," I said. "She works hard all week and likes to relax on Sunday."

My mother opened her mouth to let off another barrage, but my father said, "If it's OK with Elaine, it should be OK with us."

He told me about their plans for the time they would be in New York and said they expected me to join them. I said that was great but I had to go to work every day.

"Couldn't you get time off?" my mother said. "After all, we don't come to town that often."

"Not a chance," I said. "I'll see you for dinner and a play every night but I have to work during the day. I'm sleeping at the hotel, aren't I?"

She wasn't satisfied but she gave in.

A major snowstorm hit Manhattan next morning. Snow fell in huge globs. Manhattan was stopped in its tracks. Snowplows broke down from the weight of it and the streets were impassable. Broadway was silent, no horns, no motors, mute under its white coat, bright neon from the theatres and restaurants reflecting off the ice with an eerie glow.

My mother and father and I laughed at the stoppage of everything. We were from Chicago. We knew how to handle this weather.

We spent a hectic week, walking to plays every night, after enormous dinners. We saw "Streetcar Named Desire," starring Marlon Brando in the role he made famous, and "Member of the Wedding," with Julie Harris, and I don't remember all the rest. Ten plays in eight days. Two matinees on the weekend. What an orgy! By that time the streets were minimally passable.

What with walking to work and running around all night I didn't have the time or strength to think about the fact that Gina had left for Yale and there I was at Sadie's place, alone. Sadie had said I could stay the month of January at half-rent but that was all she could do.

I was finishing up the details of the sales program for the bride's booklet and Seymour was going on a trip across the country to sell it after the first of the year. As the only employee, I would be in charge of the office while he was gone.

He was excited about the prospects, considering the impressive results we had had in just New York and New Jersey. He had dollar signs in his eyes so I thought the time was ripe to hit him for a raise. He put me off as usual and said we would talk about it when he came back.

My parents had gone home. They had been very nice to me, taking me shopping for new clothes after work and buying me whatever I wanted. They were so transparent, especially my mother. It was a big bribe to get me to go back with them. She even offered to buy me a fur jacket if I would come back. As if I cared about a fur jacket! But we had made a sort of peace and so they left hopeful, and I stayed, relieved that they had left.

I missed Gina. She had dragged me to parties and late night gatherings with her school friends and the cast of the play, which had been given successfully at the school. This was before my parents arrived, during the pre-Christmas season. We had gone out almost every night, Gina insisting I come along.

Eric was always there, tagging after Gina. We had a great time arguing, he and I, about politics and the state of the world. We were in small groups very late at night in someone's attic apartment, lights out, candles burning, everyone smoking, and talking about books and things that mattered. It was wonderful, what I had imagined life would be like in New York.

The people, the gatherings, the conversations disappeared when Gina left. I guess she hoped I would make friends with her pals at the school and have a social life but given my tight exterior and the open and outgoing natures of the people she knew, it wasn't going to happen, and it didn't.

I called one of the girls and went out with the group once more, but they talked about their theatre work and people I didn't know. Eric wasn't with us. I felt like an outsider, a loner, which I was.

I spent a lot of time wandering around Washington Square, browsing in the used bookstores, picking up a copy of Marcel Proust's "Remembrance of Things Past," introducing myself to the works of Thomas Mann, falling in love with "Death in Venice," finding copies of Gertrude Stein, more Thomas Mann, old volumes of Ernest Hemingway.

I sat on a bench in the Square with the life of the place throbbing around me and read after work, lost in the worlds on the page. It helped ease the loneliness of Gina's absence. Sure it was cold but I dressed warmly and didn't mind, especially on weekends when the sun was shining and I should have been searching for an apartment.

From time to time I dropped into Sadie's boutique on a little street off the Square and looked through the merchandise and chatted with her. Saturdays were busy and I was happy to see the shop full of people. She catered to a clientele that was as "avant garde" as she was, so she knew what they liked.

I looked through the Times "apartment for rent" ads every day and went to see all kinds of awful places, the only ones I could afford. Then I saw an ad on the upper West Side. I had been hoping to find something in the Village but it was just too costly. The thing about the ad that intrigued me: it said the place was owned by a former dancer with Sally Rand's troupe. The rent was cheap, a room in her apartment, and she wanted a woman tenant.

I went over to see it, it was a 4th floor walkup on 100th street just off Central Park, a seedy street lined on both sides with old brownstones, some nicely kept, some run down. This building was somewhere in the middle. Joanne, the dancer, was a tall slender woman, no longer a dancer she told me because her legs had given out.

The room for rent was large, somewhat gloomy but she said I could fix it up. She said the people in the building were very nice. It was a co-op, and she would have to get approval but she didn't think there would be a problem. The best part was I could afford it.

I was approved the next day. I said goodbye to Sadie, who hugged me in a perfumed cushion-soft embrace and told me to call her if I needed anything. She said she was going to miss me. I said I would miss her but really I already missed her apartment, the fire escape where Gina and I used to sit and talk if we didn't want to be overheard, Washington Square, the bookstores, the ambiance of the neighborhood, the camaraderie of Gina and her friends that made me ache with loss.

I called Carol, Uncle George's fiancée, and told her where I was moving. We made a date to meet for lunch. I hadn't really contacted her since the night we had met at dinner. I had been too busy.

I moved into the apartment on 100th street the weekend Seymour came back from his trip and I decided there was going to be a showdown. A raise or I quit. My father had slipped me a nice check before he left without my mother knowing and that gave me the courage to make my stand.

CHAPTER 16

CO-OP

On a bright wintry Saturday at the end of January I relocated to the co-op and tried to arrange my things in the cavernous room. There was a large bed in the middle, a tall dresser on one wall, an easy chair with a lamp on another, a small bookshelf near it, and a narrow closet where I stuffed what I could.

The windows were dirty and looked out on a gangway with another building next door. It was not very bright but I didn't care, it was mine and I could afford it.

I put my little radio on top of the dresser, and turned on the opera since it was Saturday. As the room filled with "Tosca," I unpacked my things and examined the purchases I had made with my parents when they were visiting. I had worn them all, but I looked them over anyway. A black suit with a long skirt, something I had wanted since I arrived in New York. A couple of skirts and sweaters to wear to work, long skirts at last. I felt better equipped now, to handle my life, to handle Seymour, my job, and better equipped to find myself some leisure entertainment, other than reading.

As I was arranging my books on the shelf, there was a knock on the door. Joanne, asking if I would join her for lunch. How nice, I thought, flashing back to my arrival in Brooklyn and Miriam and her apartment. The kitchen, which we were going to share, was small and dingy, in fact everything in the apartment was dingy but I told myself it didn't matter. It would be fine. She mentioned that one of the neighbors, a New York City fireman who owned the second floor, was having a party for some people in the building that evening and had asked her and her new tenant if they would like to come down.

"I have another engagement," she said, "but you should definitely go. You'll find out what a friendly place this is and Al, the fireman, is a very nice fellow."

I said I would love to go and meet everyone and after lunch went back to my room to finish unpacking, feeling pretty good. Someplace to go tonight and I didn't even have to go out of the building. I started to hang up my only two paintings, prints by Diego Rivera I had bought at a small junk shop near my favorite bookstore in Washington Square.

It was terrible that they were in a junk shop, and I had rescued them with money I couldn't afford to spend. They were especially dear to me because I had rescued them and they looked great in the room, after I draped one of Uncle Sammy's afghans over the bed to brighten things up. I stepped back and observed the decor. A lot better, more cheerful, more me. Time to rest, I decided, since I wanted to make a good impression on my new neighbors. I picked up the book I was reading, sat down in the chair, and turned on the light.

Joanne had said the party was at six and not to have dinner because there would be lots of appetizers and drinks and other things to eat. As I opened my door to go downstairs, I could smell something delicious cooking.

I had dressed carefully, wearing pressed jeans and a new white shirt I had bought with my parents' money. I was thin and the jeans looked good, very New York Village.

Sounds of loud music and conversation came up the stairwell with the food smells and I hurried down, not wanting to be late. As I rounded a bend I saw the guests had spilled into the hall and across to the apartment opposite. As I hit the last step a tall rangy man with graying hair greeted me.

"Hi. Are you Joanne's new tenant?"

"Yes. I'm Elaine."

"Happy to meet you," he said, shaking my hand, "I'm Al Kelly and I live here." He pointed to the open door where sounds of Duke Ellington were streaming into the hall.

"Come and meet everybody. We all live in the building -- one happy family," he said with a short laugh. I didn't know if he was kidding but when he said family, I turned wary.

We went from one group to another and he said their names, which did not register. Mostly youngish, more men than women, a few twosomes, a couple of women who eyed me like they wanted to eat me, I stayed away from them, some other same sex couples, and Al's fireman friend Tommy, an older man, who seemed very quiet in this noisy crowd.

"I'll show you my place," Al said, leading me into his apartment. He owned the whole floor, had divided it down the middle, and made his apartment and the one across the hall into studios with small kitchens. He had a private bath. The other studio shared a bath with the one-bedroom in front. There was another one-bedroom in front of Al's place.

"This building has railroad apartments, one room leading to another, usually without a hall. I divided it so I could have income from the three rentals to pay for my studio."

Al's apartment was small but paneled in warm colored wood with a high ceiling that made it seem larger than it was. On a shelf in one corner was a television set. Nobody I knew owned a television set in 1948. A long couch stretched the length of the room, with bookcases and built-in drawers and cabinets above and around it. It was modern, clean, bright and inviting. I was amazed that a place like this could exist in a building like this.

"It's beautiful," I said, my face mirroring my surprise.

He looked around proudly. "I did it myself, with Tommy's help. We paneled the walls, did the electricity, put in the appliances, connected the TV. We made over all the apartments. The only one not finished is the studio across the hall."

He gestured out the door and I followed him into the unfinished studio. It was bare with unpainted walls and the kitchen not yet hooked up. "We'll be finishing this soon and then I'll have to get myself another tenant."

"If I hadn't just moved in, I would take it in a minute," I said, looking around. The outer wall was a giant window letting in the rising moon, the kitchen area a small alcove in one corner. A large closet in another corner gaped open without a door, not quite finished. The place was sparse, clean and seemed to be begging me to move in. I mentally started to decorate it.

Al looked at me speculatively. "There's a rumor going around that Joanne is going to sell her place and move back to California as soon as she gets a buyer. She told Gloria over there," he pointed to a large woman talking to Tommy in a corner, "that she hoped to be out soon. I don't know why she rented her place if she was going to move but this apartment will be ready in about a month, in case you want to think about it."

No sooner did I get settled than something like this happened. I had rented the room upstairs month to month, the way Joanne wanted it. Now I saw why.

"Will it be furnished?" I asked, not wanting to get saddled with more possessions than I could handle or afford.

"Sure," he said. "In fact if you wanted to move in, I'd make a special effort with the furniture."

"I'd like to see the bathroom and meet the people who would be sharing it with me."

He led the way through a closed door opposite the window wall into a small foyer where there was another closed door and a bathroom on the side wall. It was small and not too clean but seemed to have all the right equipment, a bathtub and shower included.

131

"I think Lise and Roy are at the party. Come on, I'll introduce you."

We went back through the unfinished studio. I eyed it with a proprietary glance, thinking, am I really going to do this, with my job situation so uncertain? I didn't even know how much he was charging for rent and since it was brand new it was probably going to be too much.

He led me over to a couple drinking in a corner of the hall. Lise was short and stubby, with a strong German accent, and Roy, her boyfriend, also short, worked for a publishing house. My head went up at that. We started a conversation and found out we had a lot in common. We liked the same music, read the same books and when Roy found out I wanted to be a writer, he became very interested in what I was doing.

I told him about my bride's booklet job and how I thought it was coming to an end.

"If he doesn't give me a raise the next time I ask, I'm definitely going to quit. It's a dead end anyway. The book is finished. I finished it. The promotions are all laid out. I laid them out. It's just a selling job now and I don't want to do that," I said.

I took in a sharp breath. "I can't believe I said that. I don't even have another job prospect."

Lise said, "I wouldn't worry. You have good experience now. Why don't you check the paper and see what's available before you do anything?"

Roy said, "Are you going to take the unfinished studio? We'd sure like to have you as a neighbor." Lise nodded in agreement.

More decisions. I decided to forget about it all, the job, the apartment, the moving, the unpleasant prospect of confronting Seymour when he came back from his sales trip, being jobless and moneyless, and concentrate on having a good time.

I circulated among the guests, meeting the couple, Helen and Bret, who lived in the apartment in front of Al's, a cute twosome, married, something not too many people in the building bothered with, from what I could tell. They were from South Dakota, a fact I found exotic, and had come to New York to work awhile and have a good time. We chatted and then Al served a buffet supper from his tiny kitchen, pulling out a table from the built-in wall, and we ate wherever we could find a space. I sat on the steps leading up to my place and talked with whoever came by.

I noticed a phone on the wall above my head. When I pointed it out, Al said it was for the second floor tenants.

I wasn't aware until later in the evening that I had become very friendly, a fact that made me stop and think. Maybe I was friendly all along but had never had the opportunity to show it. At Northwestern I'd been friendly but not outgoing, as I was now. I decided it was better not to think about it, just act like I felt like acting. There was no one to stop me, not any more.

The next day I arrived at the office primed for a confrontation with Seymour. I had tossed most of the night, rehearsing what I would say, bolstered by the new friends I had made, the camaraderie of Al and the other neighbors.

When I walked in the door, set my purse on the desk at the reception window-- I was the receptionist too -- I thought I wouldn't have to worry about my purse being snatched again. It had disappeared from my desk a couple of times when I went back to talk to Seymour in his office, leaving the front unguarded. The first time the police found it in a trash bin with the money gone.

Luckily I never carried more than a couple of dollars with me, mostly because I never had more than a couple of dollars at one time. The second time the police caught the thief as he was leaving the building and returned the purse to me. I carried my whole life in that purse. When it vanished I felt as though I had disappeared too. An awful feeling.

It was quiet and no smell of cigar in the air. I sat at my desk, opening the mail, waiting to pounce when Seymour walked in. After about an hour he called and said he wouldn't be in, to take care of things and he'd see me tomorrow.

I asked how his sales trip had gone and he said terrific, he'd tell me all about it when he saw me. I smiled in anticipation. I only hoped my resolve wouldn't break down.

I left early, having finished everything there was to do and went shopping for food. When I returned to the apartment, Joanne was waiting for me with a sad face.

"I have bad news. I had to sell my apartment so I could move back to Los Angeles. My mother is ill and I have to be there for a long while. I hate to leave New York but there it is. You're paid up for the month of February so you can stay until then. I'm leaving next week. The new people take it over March first."

One decision made without me doing a thing. I told Joanne not to worry. I'd just move downstairs into Al's new studio. I had no idea how to pay for it but I would find a way. Confidence in my future was something new and exciting. I wasn't even afraid after I made the decision.

I ate a hasty dinner in Joanne's kitchen, messy, with food lying around and a few roaches disappearing when the light went on, and decided I wasn't sorry to move. At least the kitchen was going to be all mine. I hurried downstairs to tell Al before he rented the place to someone else.

He was working in the apartment. I told him what had happened with Joanne, how his news had been right on target, and that I wanted to discuss renting the studio, if I could afford it.

"Great!" He climbed down from the ladder where he was doing something in the ceiling, as high as his apartment ceiling, another thing I liked about the place.

"How much are you paying upstairs?"

I told him and he said he would charge me the same thing. I was astonished. This apartment was much nicer, roomier, more liveable.

I said, "Are you sure? I'll be happy to pay it, especially if I don't have a job after tomorrow, but it seems --"

"Don't worry about it," he said. "It's worth it to me to get a tenant right away so I don't have to advertise and interview all the kooks that show up. It will be ready for you whenever you want to move in."

I could not believe my good fortune. I told him not to rush. I could stay upstairs till the end of the month but I couldn't pay him anything to secure the apartment until then.

"No problem. You just took a big weight off my shoulders. It will be a pleasure having you for a neighbor. Feel free to come down and watch my TV any time you want." Then he climbed up the ladder and disappeared into the ceiling and I left, feeling like my fairy godmother had finally shown up.

My spirits high, I called my mother that night. She seemed so happy to hear from me that I said, "Tomorrow I'm going to quit my job."

I held my breath for the tirade.

She said, "I think that's a smart move. That man has been taking advantage of your talents long enough."

I was speechless. No argument? No recrimination? No threat?

She went on, "Stay with it. I'm sure you'll find another job more to your liking. In this world we all have to take chances."

"Yes," I said, wondering at the change, "that's what I think."

We chatted a little longer and then hung up. My mother had become my friend, my encouraging friend. That night I dreamed about us having a wonderful time together in some shadowy, happy place.

Seymour was at my desk when I arrived, looking through the mail.

I had lost some of my nerve but the time was now. I had a great new place to live. I needed a great new job to go with it.

"Seymour, I have to talk to you about something important. Can we go into your office?"

He smiled and moved out of my chair. I'm sure he knew what I was going to say and he had his answer ready. It was always the same answer.

"Seymour, the bride's booklet is taking off. I've done every-thing you asked me to do, working for practically nothing, working my butt off to get this project going. And I don't have anything to show for it."

"Not true," he said. "Look at the experience you've gotten from this. Writing, dealing with customers, correspondence, things you never did before. And you owe it all to me and this job." He sat back in his chair, chewing on his cigar, his stomach sticking up over the desk, his expression complacent, daring me to disagree.

"That may be so, but I think it's time for me to move on. I think my job is finished here. The rest is sales and I don't want to do sales. I think it's time I found a place that will pay me what I'm worth."

He sat up in his chair. "You're quitting?" not believing it.

"Yes. Unless you make me a salary offer I can't refuse." I wouldn't take any offer at that point but I was enjoying watching him squirm.

"Elaine, you know we operate on a tight track here. There's very little room for extra expense."

"Yes, I know. That's why I think it's time for me to move on."

"But-- but -- you know the system, hell, you put it in. Where am I going to get someone to do the job you do? It will take months to train someone. Would you do that?"

"For $35.00 a week? I don't think so."

"You mean you're walking out now?" His face was sagging in lumps of fat, the cigar dangling.

"When I get the money you owe me for the time I worked while you were away on your trip, then I'll say good bye. And that better be by quitting time today."

He half rose. "Are you threatening me?" He tried to look menac-ing but only looked pathetic.

"No. I'm merely saying that all I want is what you owe me. "

"Don't you think you owe me something for all I did for you?"

"And what exactly is that?" I was cold as an ice cube.

He didn't answer. He opened the desk drawer, pulled out his checkbook and started writing.

"By the way," I said. "I think I deserve a bonus for this past year. You know, to show your appreciation. It has been a year that I worked for you."

I have no idea where I got the nerve to say it.

His face turned beet red. I thought he was having a stroke.

"Appreciation," he choked. "Here's what I owe you. You can leave now and don't come back." He handed me the check.

I examined it carefully, adding on my fingers to see if it was right. My math skills hadn't improved much. I pushed back my chair and moved to the door.

"Good bye, Seymour. It's been an interesting year." Before he could answer I was gone.

Walking down Lexington Avenue, I felt free. I felt proud of myself. I felt a sinking feeling that I wouldn't get a paycheck for a while. But I still had some money from the check my father had given me and now I had Seymour's check, which I hastened to the bank to deposit before he changed his mind. He had been so upset that he had written it for more than he owed me. I had my bonus after all and I didn't want him to realize it until it was too late.

After I left the bank I bought a New York Times and went home to find another job. As I walked I planned my new resume with the experience at the bride's booklet up front. I hoped any new employer wouldn't want references. Seymour was just mean enough not to give them.

Job-hunting, via the New York Times, was not easy. Writing jobs were found by first submitting a letter and a resume to some box number, and then waiting for a call or a letter to invite you in for an interview. I scoured the help wanted pages every day sending off letters by the dozen, with only rejections in response, that is, when they answered at all.

Joanne had moved out and it was very spooky up there without her or any furniture in the rest of the apartment. I waited anxiously for Al to finish the studio so I could move down into civilization.

It was a good time to move since I wasn't doing anything except answering ads.

I finally found a temporary job doing research for a magazine publishing company thinking about starting a women's magazine. The research would show what interest they could expect and also what kinds of articles they had to plan. It paid something, not much, but there was the chance that if the magazine started up, they might give me a job. I spent a lot of time at the library filling out the research cards and sending them in.

At one point Al said I could move. Everything was connected and he had put in a bed, which I could make into a couch if I wanted to. The next weekend I moved downstairs, Al helping me carry things. He really was a nice man.

The studio, bright and clean, was painted a very light blue, my favorite color. The single bed rested against one wall, and a wooden table with two chairs stood near the tiny kitchen, which had a new stove and oven, a new sink and a new very small refrigerator. I loved it immediately, and fixed up the bed to look like a couch, Uncle Sammy's afghan coming in handy again. I decided to buy colorful sheets to make into drapes for the window. I had the money from my research job.

The food from Joanne's refrigerator filled the new one but I went out to buy other things. I came back with milk cartons to use as bookcases, almost as important as a dresser, which I did not have. I used milk cartons for my clothes too, putting them in the closet, where there was more room than I needed.

That evening I had finished. The sheets at the window were pastel striped and draped nicely over curtain rods already installed. I had arranged my books in the plastic milk cartons, which were different colors: red, white, light blue, dark blue and black. I even had a small vase full of daisies for my table. The radio was playing a waltz. I could not believe my good fortune, to be living there. I'd get a job soon, I knew it.

My door was open and Al came in to see how I was doing. He was very pleased with the way things looked and said he was going to get me a dresser, a chair and a reading lamp, "since you're such a bookworm."

I invited him to stay for dinner but he was on his way to the firehouse for his shift. He said he would be back in two days.

"You can use my place while I'm gone. Until you get a chair, come in and read or watch TV. All my tenants have that privilege." He showed me how to open the door.

A couple of weeks later, the publishing company said they didn't need any more research because they had decided not to go ahead with the magazine.

I walked around to various places checking the personnel departments, answering ads, but with no luck. I was getting desperate, the sinking feeling in my stomach a permanent thing, when I saw an ad for a comic book company looking for an editor. I sent a resume, thinking it was a dead end but I had to try everything.

In the days that followed, after answering any ad that seemed promising, I stretched out on my bed-couch to read Proust's "Swann's Way." A good time to read it. Time was stretching endlessly.

One afternoon while I was deep into the masterwork, somewhere in the French countryside, unable to put down the book since I had started it, Lise stuck her head in my door.

"Phone call, Elaine," she said.

Who would call me, except my mother? I went to the phone to tell her the latest. But it was the comic book publisher asking me to come in for an interview the next day.

CHAPTER 17

THE COMICS

Winner Comics was located near 34th street and Broadway. As I opened the door, my fingers were crossed. I had to get the job. My money was almost gone. I had to pay Al the next month's rent. He had been letting me live rent free up to now and I was determined not to take advantage.

A man met me at the door and ushered me into the office of Hap Armbruster, the publisher, a stubby man with a red face and a ring of whitish hair around the crown of his head. He motioned me to a chair without looking up from the papers he was holding. I realized he was studying my resume.

"It says here you graduated from Northwestern's journalism school. That's a pretty powerful credential. It also says you were in the journalism honorary society." He looked up, staring me in the face for the first time, smiling with a little twist to his lips.

"Yes," I answered as businesslike as I could manage, since I was shaky and my stomach was churning. At least he liked something.

"You may not think that these credentials are necessary for working on comic books but we run a very tight ship here," he said, leaning back and crossing his arms. "I, especially, am particular about spelling and grammar and punctuation. In the comics we have a lot of punctuation, you know. This other experience wouldn't do you any good here," he said, waving a hand at the resume.

So much for the bride's booklets. "I do a lot of writing on my own," I said, hoping to impress.

"Really. Maybe you'd like to do freelancing for some of the comics."

"I need a full-time job. I could do that in addition."

"That's what I like. Someone who's not afraid to work. The pay is $75.00 to start. Could you begin tomorrow? Or do you need time to think it over."

"W-well--" I couldn't get the word "yes" out.

"We have a couple of other prospects who've been interviewed, but I think you have better credentials." He paused.

"I'll do it," I blurted.

"Good. I'll introduce you to the editor you'll be working with."

He picked up the phone and soon the man who had ushered me into the office opened the door.

"This is Carl Kahn." I was introduced as the new assistant. Carl Kahn was about middle age, with dark hair and an ambling gait that seemed to say, "Don't rush me."

"Show Elaine around," Hap Armbruster said. Then he turned to me. "Carl will tell you what you'll be doing. See you tomorrow." He shook my hand and swiveled his chair around so his back faced us.

Outside Hap's office, Carl Kahn looked me over with interest. "You must have had some resume," he said. "I didn't think I was ever going to get another assistant. Come on. I'll take you to your office."

"You mean I have an office all to myself?"

"Sure. You're an editor, aren't you? You'll have to talk to writers who come up to visit. Or complain." He flashed a grin.

We went into a spacious room with a window in one corner looking out on the street below, letting in the sun. A desk stood against the wall, piled with papers. I wondered if the papers were for me. Next to the window was an artist's table raised at an angle with a high stool in front of it. The walls were lined with framed photos of comic book covers: cartoon characters, adventure figures, a few romance drawings with couples in a clinch.

"These are the comic books, right?"

"Yep. We do Manley Mouse who you see there," he pointed to a cartoon. "We do an action figure, you know, like a takeoff of Superman, called the Question Mark, champion of the people." He gestured at a muscular figure in black tights with a big red question mark on his chest. "And we have a line of romance comics," pointing to the couples. "There are other books with other heroes. You'll learn about them all, since you'll be reading the scripts before we buy them."

"I will?"

"Yep. Part of the job. At first we'll oversee the process until you get the hang of it. You'll also be correcting storyboards, drawings on boards like this."

He pulled a large cardboard divided into squares out of the corner and placed it on the artist's table.

"You'll be checking the lettering inside the conversation balloons to make sure the spelling is okay. Hap is a nut about spelling. As if the people who read these things care about spelling."

A hint of sarcasm? I was beginning to like Carl.

"How do I correct the spelling?"

"With this." He handed me a white pencil for whiting out the offending letter or word then a black pen to letter in the correct spelling.

"Looks like fun."

"That's a good attitude. Keep thinking it's fun and you'll enjoy working here. Just take a tip from me. Turn down any invitations from Hap to go out to lunch. Out to lunch means drinking."

"I'm -- I'm -- not sure --"

"Don't worry, he won't ask you, not for a while. But when Hap drinks he goes overboard, promises the moon. That's why we have to keep getting new assistants. He takes them out to lunch, raises their salaries so high when he gets sloshed that the big shots who run the corporation get mad and fire the assistants. Just a word to the wise."

He shook my hand. "A pleasure to meet you. See you tomorrow." He ambled away, leaving me to find my way out the door.

My office was off a large room where people were working on storyboards, typing, talking on the phone. Busy. I couldn't wait to get started.

My head was whirling as I walked to the bus stop. I had a job. A job that paid money! So what if it was for the comic books. I wasn't exactly a literary giant. Besides it sounded like fun. And maybe it could lead to better things. As I rode to my stop on the bus, I was so relieved that my money problems were solved I forgot about how lonely I had been feeling, the persistent ache near my heart.

That night everyone came crowding into my apartment to find out what had happened at the interview, Al and Tommy, Lise and Roy, the couple from South Dakota - Helen and Bret. When I told them I had been hired on the spot they hugged me and congratulated me and Al went to his apartment and brought back a bottle of wine that he insisted we share in a toast to my new job.

I was dazed with all the good feeling until Lise asked, "Where exactly is this new job?"

"It's for a comic book company. I thought you knew."

She had a peculiar expression on her face. "No, no I didn't. Are you sure you want this job? It's so -- so -- déclassé."

"Lise!" Roy exclaimed. "That's not nice. It's not like Elaine's going into the Mafia. It's a perfectly legal job."

"I know," Lise said. "Forgive me, Elaine." But after that she had a fishy look on her face whenever I talked to her, as if I didn't know anything because I worked for the comics.

After everyone left, Roy came back. "I hope you weren't too mad at Lise for what she said. She's German, you know, and she thinks that any written word must be "literary," Thomas Mann or nothing. Being in publishing like I am, I know the truth of it, that the comic book mentality usually outvotes the literary except in certain small exclusive circles, which Lise thinks she's a part of."

"That's okay, Roy. Actually, it's the way I think too. But it didn't stop me from taking the job. Does that make me a hypocrite?"

"Not at all. It depends on whether you want to eat regularly. I have the same problem. I don't work for the comics, which are up front in what they offer to the public. But the stuff we publish isn't much better. Lise and I don't discuss these things much. By the way, have you started writing anything? That's one way to counter-act negative publicity."

"I don't care about negative publicity. I don't care what Lise or anyone else thinks. I do what I need to do, or what I want to do. I don't pretend to be anything other than a person trying to figure out her place in the scheme of things."

We shook hands, Roy holding my hand longer than necessary. Then he left, with me thinking what a nice person he was, too nice for a shit like Lise.

I wondered what Gina would say about my new job with her high standards of theatre and literature. Probably the same thing Lise had said. Gina's friends would agree.

It just wasn't fair! No sooner did something positive happen to me, something I delighted in and felt good about, than the negative side would rise up and bite me. I wouldn't listen to the negatives. I would collect my outrageous paycheck and live a better life. I might even sit down one day and start to write stories again. But I had a sneaking feeling that the stories would be scripts for the comics, to make even more money.

I dressed carefully the next morning in my black suit with the long skirt, determined to make a good impression. As I rode the bus with others on their way to work, the sun was shining, it was unseasonably warm and my spirits were high.

Carl Kahn was at his desk when I walked in and passed his open door. He waved and I looked around the big room, which was already bustling. I entered my office with a newfound sense of belonging. I was an editor, I didn't even care of what.

I sat down at the desk, turned on the lamp and began to look over the papers on the desk. They were all manuscripts, laid out in play format, dialog lines with directions in between. I flashed back to when I was small, playing with my paper dolls and making up fantastic stories for my little people. I guessed these stories wouldn't be too different.

The first one was an action script for the Question Mark. I read through it swiftly, thinking this stuff wasn't bad at all, true comic book writing with the oofs and ahhs and clonks and other sound effects, but the story was pretty good.

Carl ambled through the open door. "Ah, I see you've started right in. Good. Hap will like that. We do everything we can to keep Hap calm. He has a very short fuse, as I hope you never find out. What's that you're reading?" He leaned over to see.

"A script for the Question Mark." I showed him.

"Actually, you're not supposed to be doing that just yet. I don't know how the script got on your desk but I'll take it. Did you read it?"

"Yes," I said, disappointed that I wasn't to be trusted yet.

"What did you think?"

"Well, considering that it's an action script for kids, I would imagine, it's not bad. There are a few grammatical mistakes, some misspellings, but the gist of it is exciting and well plotted. I liked it. I would buy it if I had the call."

"Good. You'll be getting that authority sooner rather than later."

Hap walked in. "Hard at work already. Good."

Carl told him about the script I had just read and what I thought. He smiled and nodded his head. "That's just what I want from you. Read a few more and come into my office and tell me what you think." He left before I could answer.

"Keep it up," Carl said under his breath. "You're making a good impression. If there's something you don't like, tell him."

"Don't worry," I said. "I always do."

The days at Winner Comics became a routine of reading manu-scripts, talking them over with Carl and then Hap, if it was a question of buying them or not, most scripts not worthy of discussion and sent back with a printed rejection. I became familiar with the writers who had the boss's favor, the ones who wrote for the most popular books, the ones to be handled with kid gloves.

They would call me on the phone if I offered suggestions in the margin on how to improve the story or if there were excessive corrections to the grammar, or sometimes just to talk. Most conversations were pleasant but some were shouting matches, with me listening as they shouted.

"What do you mean, the ending doesn't work!" one writer yelled into the phone as soon as I picked it up. He obviously didn't care who was on the other end of the line.

I asked politely who it was and what his problem was. Using a soft voice and a nice manner, I usually calmed them down pretty fast. But this one was really irate. You'd think I had butchered "War and Peace" to hear him complain. I gave him a couple of suggestions on how to get the ending more exciting and more believable and told him to rewrite according to the suggestions in the margins and resubmit.

I said, "I'll get to it as soon as I receive it. Thank you for your interest. It was very helpful of you to call." We hung up as friends.

One of the most popular comic books was a soldier of fortune magazine, adventure stories in deserts, jungles or other exotic locations with mercenaries fighting enemies of the good guys. One of the writers was a pet of Hap's. He could do no wrong. I was told -- Carl said it with emphasis -- not to reject one of his stories without getting an okay from Hap.

I read a few of his scripts. I didn't think they were that great, mostly I didn't like his politics, coming through loud and clear. He was somewhere to the right of Hitler. Not my kind of guy.

There was a huge pileup of reading. I was going through the scripts at top speed, rejecting right and left, not noticing who the

writers were, just sending back the garbage. One of them was especially awful, not only badly written but stupid and contrived in plot
and resolution.

A week later, Hap came storming into my office his face redder
than usual.

"Did you reject a story of Shawn Martin's? Against my express
orders?"

"Um- uh- not that I know of. But I had a huge pile of scripts to
go through and I didn't check the writers' names. Did I do that?"

"You sure did, and now he's coming in here like a thunderbolt
to confront you face to face. I just got off the phone with him. You
better fix this up. He has too big a following to lose him." He turned
abruptly and left, leaving me shaking in my chair.

Shawn Martin. Of all the writers, he was the one I wanted to
meet the least. I took deep breaths and hoped I could talk myself
out of this one. I could see my job vanishing through the open
window.

Carl appeared, looking concerned. "Elaine, you sure put your
foot in a pile of shit! Are you going to be able to handle this?"

"Hey, remember you said my office would be used for writers
visiting or complaining? Well, one of the complainers is coming
and I'll take care of it." I sounded more confident than I felt.

"Okay, when he gets here, he'll have to go by my office. I'll
stay in the background in case you need help. He's a real mean son
of a bitch."

"I figured that. I'll be okay." I hoped Shawn Martin wasn't
armed like his heroes, guns in belts, knives in boots, poison in
pockets. One of Shawn's nastier attributes was the way he portrayed
women -- submissive to the will of men or as monsters out to get
them.

Shortly before lunch I heard a loud voice in the outer office and
then Hap greeting someone. No doubt who it was. Hap came into
my office with a large man in boots and a cowboy hat and a huge
frown on his face. A John Wayne clone, carrying the rejected manuscript rolled up like a weapon.

"Elaine," Hap said, smiling nervously, "I'd like you to meet Shawn Martin, one of our most valued writers."

I stood up and shook his hand. It was like a steel vice but I pressed back and tried not to flinch. I smiled brightly and said, "Very happy to meet you. I've enjoyed reading your stories. In fact I look forward to them."

He sat down in the chair next to my desk, looking uncertain. I guess he didn't expect a small young person who would look him right in the eye. He acted like he expected people to be afraid when they met him. But here was this female, complimenting him after rejecting his story.

Hap said, "I'll leave you two to talk things over," and he walked out after giving me a look - *fix it or else.*

"So, little lady," I hated when people called me that, "what exactly made you send this back?" He tossed the script on the desk in front of me.

"Mr. Martin, the stories I've read of yours are so much better than this one." He frowned and started to say something. I hurried on. "I know you wouldn't want to disappoint your loyal fans, we wouldn't want to disappoint your loyal fans. And this manuscript just doesn't live up to the standards you have set for yourself."

"And who made you the judge of my standards?" he thundered.

I saw Carl outside my office about to come in. I shook my head slightly and he stopped.

"It's my job." I said. "I can't accept anything that doesn't measure up to your past examples of excellence. But that doesn't mean," I said hurriedly when I saw him turning even redder, "but that doesn't mean we can't fix this and make it the best you've done so far. It really won't take much, if you're willing to go for it."

"What do you suggest?" he said, with more menace than willingness.

I picked up the script and went through it, offering ideas for better conflicts, better denouements, and a socko ending that made him break into a big grin. Along the way I changed some of the clichés, hoping he wouldn't blow up. I kept my voice soft, my manner soothing.

"Little lady, I like it. I'll take this home and do a rewrite. You were right. I knew this wasn't as good when I sent it in but I thought I'd get away with it. I always did with Carl." He winked. "Don't tell him I said so."

"For sure." I smiled in relief.

Hap came in to see how it was going.

"Great little editor," Martin boomed. "She fixed the thing up."

"Let's go to lunch," Hap said. "We can talk about it. Want to come, Elaine? We'd love to have you."

I remembered what Carl had said about lunch with Hap and answered, "Thanks but I brought my lunch. There's too much to finish here. I can read while I eat."

Hap smiled. "Okay. Maybe some other time." The two of them walked out of my office. I collapsed into my chair.

Carl ambled in. "Hey, Elaine. They could use you at the United Nations as a mediator."

"If I don't have a heart attack first. Now if you'll excuse me I'm having my lunch and relaxing." I pulled the lunch bag from my desk, my hands still trembling.

"Right. I'm gone."

Thank God. I took a long drink of soda to calm myself. I was sure to notice the names of the writers I rejected after that.

I spent mornings reading scripts, making a pile to be discussed later with Carl, another pile rejected by me. I was busy with this until lunchtime, scanning one script after the other, papers flying as I went through the stories. They were a quick read and I could easily visualize them coming to life on the page as I speed-read. If I couldn't visualize them, they were gone.

After lunch was my favorite time of the day. I sat at my artist's table and corrected storyboards. On a nice day, the sun streamed in, I cracked the window, and sounds of New York traffic filled the room. Something about the tactile feel of the white-out pen and the black ink making the corrections gave me a sense of participating in a different creative act, contributing my bit to the whole enterprise. As I whited out and inked in, I was as happy as a kid doing arts and crafts.

Each storyboard covered the surface of the artist's table, divided, for the most part, into six squares containing the drawings, oversized, dramatic, exciting, as the action figures literally leaped from their frames. It was easy to see that some of the artists had talent, probably did fine art on the side and drew for the comics to make a living. The cartoon characters were not as dramatic but were as lively as Disney, and the romance drawings, though I would gag regularly at the scripts, were pretty good, like comic strips in the Sunday papers.

Most of the drawings were done freelance, the artists assigned a script to pencil in the preliminary sketches. After they were okayed, they were sent back to the artist to be inked in and colored, then returned for final approval, usually by Hap, who had the last say on everything.

There were a few artists on staff who inked in and colored the drawings the original artist was too busy to finish, or in case of emergency when someone blew an assignment, to complete it before deadline. Jim, the head man in this department, sat at his table, hair falling in his eyes, heavy glasses falling down his nose, peering at storyboards all day. No wonder he had a permanent stoop.

After the storyboards were corrected I gave them to Jim, who looked up and took them with a smile. He always had a good word about my work and said I should take up drawing. I tried not to laugh, and said I couldn't draw a straight line. But words, words were different and had to be correct. In that I agreed with Hap.

Late in the afternoon I went to Carl's office with the scripts to be discussed. Many of these were really terrible but I brought them in because I knew they were the stuff he liked, especially the romances. Besides I wasn't going to make another Shawn Martin mistake. Mostly we agreed on the ones that were good and argued about the ones that were bad. Those were the ones, especially the ones by Hap's pets, that sent us to Hap's office and he decided. It was a pretty good system, kept me off the hook.

After the end of one of these sessions, Hap said, "Elaine, I've got an additional job for you. Carl and I were thinking, these romance books are really taking off, the market is mostly teen-age girls and I think we need to give them something more."

"Like what," I said, the romance books being my absolutely least favorite.

"We were thinking an advice to the lovelorn column where the readers could write letters about their romantic problems and we would answer them in print. How does that sound?"

"Depends on who's going to do it."

Hap laughed. "I think you'd be perfect for the job. You're young, pretty, must have some experience in your background, you don't need much, believe me, and we would monitor the letters and take out the raunchiest ones."

"Why do you think they'd be raunchy?"

Carl said, "You should see some of the letters we get about the stories in those books."

"Can I see them, to give me an idea of what to expect?"

Hap roared. "My God Elaine! What a thought! We throw them away they're so awful. I promise you won't get any letters like that. Carl will see to it."

So I was going to write a column on love problems, what a laugh! With censored letters. My imagination was really going to get a workout.

"You able to do it?" Hap said, his expression canceling out any negative answer.

"I'll do my best, but romantic problems aren't my strong suit." Figuring they'd better know in advance.

"You'll do fine," Carl said. "You have a problem, just call me. The announcement is going into Real Romances next issue so be prepared for the mail next month. I have to go home now. My kid is in a game tonight and I promised him I'd be there." He ambled out and I started to leave.

"Are you okay with this, Elaine?" Hap said. "I don't want you to do anything that makes you uncomfortable."

"It's okay."

"Attagirl!" He patted my shoulder as I left.

My thoughts were back at the office as I let myself into my apartment. I had no idea what problems would be presented to me by this new turn of events. I was sure my ignorance was going to come out big time. The nervous twitch in my stomach was more than hunger.

I pulled out a leftover casserole, put it in the oven to heat, then lay down on my couch-bed and picked up the Proust. I was almost finished with the first volume. I doubted there would be any insight into my dilemma from reading Proust, but I needed to escape.

It was March and an early spring. Warm air came in my open window along with New York soot. Lise was playing German lieder on her record player. I could hear it through my closed door. I always kept the door closed between our apartments, even when the door to the outer hall was open.

There was a knock and Roy came in, the music blasting behind him.

"How's it going?" he said, pulling out a chair near the table.

He seemed to have appointed himself my guardian, looking in on me every few days. I didn't tell him how impatient this made me, how I had hated being looked after my whole life. But he was such a nice person, and I didn't think he was having an easy time with Lise, so I just let it ride.

"It's going pretty well but I have a new wrinkle," I said, putting down my book. I told him about the lovelorn column and he broke into a grin.

"I can imagine what you're going to get. From Appalachia and every hick town from here to the West Coast. What material! You won't have an excuse not to start writing after that."

"Roy, why are you pushing? Don't you know that when I'm ready to start, I'll start, without any prompting?" I sounded more irritated than I felt. I really liked Roy. If he had been better looking, I don't know what would have happened. He was short which made me feel short, his complexion was awful, acne plus, and he wore thick glasses. I guess he reminded me of myself when I was younger, a self I had been trying to bury. But he was a lot sweeter and more compassionate that I had ever been.

Just then my oven buzzer went off and I invited him to share my dinner, to show there were no hard feelings. Lise poked her head in and said she was leaving for her meeting. Roy waved goodbye.

He said, "I have an open bottle of really good wine." Before I could stop him he ran next door and came back with a bottle of Chianti.

"You didn't have to do that. It's just a tuna casserole."

As we ate and drank we chatted about our different jobs and then I asked what kind of a meeting Lise was going to. He said she belonged to this literary group affiliated with the bookstore she worked at and once a week she had to lead discussions of books the people had read.

"That sounds like fun."

"Not to hear her tell it. She thinks the people are all morons and half of them don't even read the books. She asks these questions that only an English lit major can understand. Most of the people are housewives from the neighborhood and don't know what she's talking about. I've gone to a few of them with her but they turn into the two of us arguing about the book and the others sitting and listening with their mouths open."

Laughing, I said, "How did you two get together?"

"Last year I wandered into the bookstore and was searching for a particular magazine. She helped me find it, I thought she was cute, asked her out for coffee after work, and we talked almost the whole night. I was coming out of an unhappy relationship and was lonelier than I thought. She didn't believe in relationships but I got her to change her mind. You know how it goes."

Actually I didn't know at all, but I wasn't going to admit it.

Dinner was over and I started to wash the dishes. He carried the plates to the sink and stood very near. "You must know, Elaine, how much I like you."

I froze. Quick! A letter to the lovelorn column. "What do I do?"

I turned to wipe off the table. "I like you too but we are neighbors and friends and you have another obligation. Even though I'm not as crazy about your obligation as you are, I don't believe in taking up with someone else's guy."

His shoulders drooped and he said he had to be up early. He took his bottle of wine and left.

I picked up my book but couldn't read. I had come to New York to find out about life and every time it came too near I backed off. I was probably the only virgin over twenty in the city of New York.

A new man had moved in next door, the couple from South Dakota having gone back home so Bret could work for his father and Helen could have a baby. I missed them, they were so cute. Every time they were going to have sex they announced, "We're going to make love. Nobody come in." It was the only time they closed their door. But about ten minutes later they were back, flushed and smiling. Pretty quick, I thought, but since I had no idea how long it took, never having done it, I just smiled back.

The new neighbor, Howie, was in import-export, unmarried, tall and well built with brown wavy hair, a longish thin nose and a mustache. He looked like John Barrymore but sounded like George Raft. He started flirting the minute we were introduced by Al, who liked his tenants to be friendly.

What about Al? Al liked men better than women, I found out, Tommy his main man. They were firemen, the epitome of macho and maleness, but it didn't carry over into their sex lives and I guess it didn't matter much, at least to me.

As I sat on the couch wondering how I could change my life, get more experience so I could succeed at this lovelorn column, I decided love was going to have to wait. I would carry on without it.

Howie might be the best candidate. He was available, definitely ready and, to hear him tell it, seemed to have a lot of experience with sex. It would be a good learning experience, I told myself. But I decided to get drunk first.

The following week I invited Howie for dinner and he accepted eagerly. We had scotch before dinner, killed a very large bottle of wine during dinner, and I had bought a small bottle of cordial for afterward.

We were on the couch, smooching, I never served the cordial and the next thing I knew, I was very drunk and so was he, and we did it. It took a lot longer than ten minutes and, thinking it over later, wasn't too unpleasant. He staggered out about midnight, saying he was going to pass out and wanted to be in his own bed. I agreed, ready to pass out myself.

I took a long shower to sober up, and thought about the whole event, what I could remember, feeling pretty smug. I was now ready to face the world and the column. I had accomplished what I had sought to do without love messing up the picture. I didn't plan on doing it with Howie again, though, no matter what he thought.

CHAPTER 18

THE END OF IT ALL

I started to spend a lot of time at Al's place when he wasn't home. His couch was comfortable, the light was good for reading, and the surroundings more luxurious than mine. I had put Proust aside for a while and was deep into a book by Simone de Beauvoir about her affair with Andre Gide. Then Howie came in and said he wanted to watch Milton Berle. Did I want to watch with him?

Not really, but I didn't want to seem unfriendly after the other night. I said okay as he turned on the TV. We chatted, both uncomfortable, and then he said abruptly, "Hey, I feel bad about what happened. I guess I got carried away." He always talked out of the side of his mouth.

"That's okay. So did I. But we can be friends anyway, can't we?"

His face lit up in a grin. "Great! I thought you would be mad."

"Nope."

Then the program came on and we watched Berle's shenanigans and I was hit with a great idea, an idea for a script for the comic book Manley Mouse with a radio comic named Hilton Squirrel. I couldn't wait to get started, so I said good night to Howie and went next door where I pulled out the small portable typewriter I had asked my mother to bring when she visited New York, set it on the table and started to write.

I knew the format and knocked out a script in a couple of hours. I couldn't wait to see Carl's face when I gave it to him the next day.

He was delighted and took it to Hap's office, who came rushing in a while later as I was reading at my desk and said, "Elaine! This is great! We're going to make it the lead story in the next issue. I've already ordered the cover. You're going to get a nice check for this."

I was so elated. My first sale. It was like I had written a best seller. I decided to try my luck with some of the other books. Besides the cartoons, the only books not preempted by Hap's pets were romance comics, which I hated. But maybe if I wrote some of them, I could make them better. My newly experienced sexual adventure had given me more confidence, though it hadn't exactly been earthshaking.

Shortly after the manuscript sale, the mail for the lovelorn column started to pour in. I walked into my office one morning and there were boxes piled all over the floor.

I ran to Carl's office. "I thought you were going to read some of those letters. I can't do anything else, from the look of it."

"Calm down. You have a whole month to answer them. And you don't have to answer them all, just the ones that will make a good column." He leaned back in his chair. "I glanced through some of them and they're pretty much alike. You can choose a representative few and answer them all that way."

I was feeling grumpy as I went back to my office, vowing the letters would not interfere with the things I liked to do.

That afternoon, curiosity took over. I finished the storyboards early, and started on a box of letters. I whipped through about twenty of them before I was ready to gag. It seemed everyone had the same problems with their boyfriends, who only wanted to do IT and the girls wanted me to tell them if IT was all right, if they should wait, what to do.

My God! I was totally unequipped to advise teenagers on such serious things. If I told them to abstain they would think I was an old prune and not listen. If I told them to go for it, the pregnancy rate would shoot up and it would be my fault! This would take some tact, some roundabout writing, some heavy thinking.

I decided to sleep on it and start answering them the next day. I could fit three or four letters in one column. If I read till I found suitable ones, I could write the thing and have it off my back for one whole month.

The column was called "Ask Margo," and was placed in a particularly obnoxious comic book, the stories awful, the drawings not as good as some of the others.

Hap had hired another assistant, a woman with graying hair and a cigarette always in her mouth. She had a low whiskey voice and seemed pretty confident. We struck up an acquaintance, I can't call it a friendship, because there was something about her I didn't trust. I was thinking she might be able to help with the letters but Hap put her in the main office, reading scripts, "to take some of the load off of you," he said to me one day. Her name was Amy.

We went out to lunch from time to time and she told me how she had been knocking around New York for a while, trying to get a job and this seemed like a good one. I agreed. I agreed with everything she said. Somehow I felt that she was a spy set there to watch me. Paranoia creeping in. She drank a lot while we ate and I figured she would be a good candidate for one of Hap's lunches.

I knocked out the first column after picking the most articulate letters and the ones with different problems. Some had trouble with their families, some had trouble at school and some had the generic problem of doing IT. I was careful. I never said what they should do. I gave examples of other behaviors that might apply. Hap thought it was good and so I was okay for that month.

About then I started turning out scripts freelance, encouraged by the first script's success. I did a few romances and then I tried an action story, breaking in on Hap's sacred cows. He had accepted everything up to then. I was making a lot of money and putting it in the bank, saving up for a trip to France, my lifelong dream.

Ever since I had read "The Three Musketeers" and the other Dumas stories, I had wanted to go to France. Now, reading the Proust and de Beauvoir, I wanted to travel in France more than ever. To walk the streets the characters walked, visit the castles where they had fought and loved, sit in the cafes where they mulled the ideas of the world. And if I kept writing and selling, I might have enough saved up by early fall.

Hap came into my office with my action script in his hand.

"Elaine, how come you decided to write this? It's very good, very exciting, calls for great action drawings, but why?"

"I don't know. Change of pace?" That wasn't the reason at all. The action scripts paid the most and if I could get some cover stories, it would almost clinch my trip.

"Well," he paused. "I'll accept this one because we're short in one book, but don't do any more. Stick to the romances. You do those best."

I stared at his retreating back, watching my trip follow him out the door. No matter. I would just write more of the others to make up the difference.

I had been getting in touch with my parents a lot lately. They liked to hear about my exploits in the comic book industry and were very proud of my success. And I felt a lot more confident by then, able to carry on a conversation with my mother without feeling she was going to order me around. She called more and more often and we chatted as if we were friends, not mother and daughter, which I found exhilarating. It made me feel accepted, included, especially when she approved of everything I was doing. What a difference from the old days! She even asked my opinion on some things. For the first time in my life I felt close to her.

I didn't mention my interlude with Howie, knowing her ideas on that subject, her reluctance to discuss anything related to sex.

Carol, Uncle George's fiancée, had gone back to Chicago to marry him. She called before she left and I told her I was sorry

I would miss the wedding. I wished her the best, happy it wasn't happening to me.

Carl was going on vacation and I was taking over his job for the week he would be gone. Amy was going to be my helper. It was very exciting to be the boss and I concentrated on doing the best job I could. I worked with Hap on script selection and Amy took over most of the storyboard corrections. I was sorry to let that job go even though I knew I'd get it back when Carl returned.

Hap and I were working closely and then one day he said, "Come on, Elaine. Let's go to lunch."

My heart stopped. I didn't know what to say. It was too sudden. I had no excuse. I couldn't just refuse. I decided I would try my best to control the situation. Confidence in myself was never higher.

"Okay, Hap," I said. "But there's a lot left to do."

"You know Elaine, you're a real workhorse. Lighten up. Let's have some fun."

Fun to Hap was getting as drunk as possible in the shortest possible time.

We walked to his favorite watering hole and before we were seated, there was a double scotch at his plate.

"What are you drinking?" he said as the waiter stood poised.

"Ginger ale?"

He let out a hoot. "What a kidder! Bring her the same." He pointed to his glass.

"With lots of ice," I interjected, reaching for a large roll. I figured I'd better coat my stomach as fast as possible.

By the time my drink arrived, Hap had finished his and ordered another.

This went on for a few rounds. I was sipping as slowly as I could, hoping he would do the same, but he was well on his way and not noticing how much I was consuming. I was getting dizzy, the room was turning slowly. I figured if I had one more, I'd fall off my chair.

"Hap, I'm starving. Let's order." I was on my third drink, he was on his sixth and getting happier by the minute.

"Anything for my favorite editor," he sloshed, and called over the waiter for some menus.

I ordered a hamburger, but halfway through the meal I had to excuse myself to go to the ladies room and throw up. I wondered if I would survive the day.

Holding on to the wall, I made my way back to the table to find that Hap had had the dishes cleared, and ordered Drambuie for us, a sweet cordial he especially liked.

"Elaine," he said, raising his glass, "I'm going to propose a toast. Here's to an editor who's going to get a big reward."

"What reward?" I muttered, my tongue feeling like a foreign object.

"I'm raising your salary, doubling it." He smiled a satisfied smile, and downed his glass.

"Come on," he said. "Drink up to celebrate your raise."

"No, Hap, please don't." He must have heard the desperation in my voice but he ignored it.

"You're paying me more than enough already." I was almost in tears. I couldn't think in my muddled condition, but I knew things were out of control.

"I believe in people getting paid well for good work." He set his jaw stubbornly and started on his second Drambuie, mine waiting at my plate. I had hardly touched the first one.

If I kept objecting, his good humor could turn sour and he might fire me on the spot. If I accepted the raise there was always the chance the big guys in Corporate would go along with it, or maybe Carl could fix it when he came back. The options seemed better if I went along.

I raised my glass. "Thank you very much," and downed it at a gulp, feeling it burn itself into the lining of my already aching stomach.

Then I had to excuse myself again. My insides were doing a flipflop and I barely made it to the ladies room. Hap hardly noticed

I was gone. As I staggered away he was ordering another, his face beaming with good feelings at his generosity and high spirits. Very high spirits.

He paid the bill and I said I didn't feel well and asked if I could have the afternoon off. He patted me on the shoulder in concern and said sure, I could. I had worked enough that day. He tottered down the street toward the office, humming a happy tune and I caught the first bus home.

Carl came back to work the next week and it wasn't long before he ambled into my office, his face expressionless.

"Did you go out to lunch with Hap while I was gone?" He lounged into the chair near my desk.

"Carl, I couldn't get out of it. He insisted. I was working constantly with him while you were gone. What happened? I don't like the way you look."

"Remember what I told you when you first came to work here? About the assistants? About the bosses upstairs? Well, they got a load of the salary Hap boosted you up to and had a fit. So I guess this is goodbye."

I sat there, I had been expecting it, I had hoped it wouldn't happen, and there it was. I was about to be unemployed, my trip to France another busted dream. Worse, though, was the fact that I really liked working at Winner Comics. No matter how déclassé Lise thought it was, it was fun and profitable. You couldn't ask more from a job.

"When do I have to go?" I was trying hard not to cry at the unfairness of the trap that had caught me.

"You have two weeks notice and you get severance pay, a week's salary, the old salary." He was getting up. I tried one more time.

"Isn't there anything you can do? Tell the bosses it was a mistake. I'd be happy to work for my old salary. I never asked for the raise. I don't even want it."

"Too late. You should have done something sooner. Amy is getting your job."

I knew it. I was screwed in all directions. There was nothing for me to do but swallow and take it.

"Can I still write scripts freelance?" hanging on to whatever I could.

"Oh, sure. That would be fine. Hap loves your stories. He would be happy if you did write some freelance. He might not feel so guilty. I'm sorry it had to end this way. But you know, I warned you."

The next two weeks were a nightmare. Hap never appeared. Jim, the storyboard man, told me how sorry he was to see me leave. The girls in the office chipped in and bought me a plant. I turned over the lovelorn letters to Amy, the one thing I wasn't sorry to give up. I loved the disgust on her face when she looked at them.

"Have fun," I said dropping the boxes on her desk, one by one.

"As long as you're still here, would you help me with these?"

"Nope. I'm leaving today."

It was Friday and Carl had paid me, not saying much, and I walked out of Winner Comics for the last time.

Back at the co-op, everyone commiserated with me and I started to think about another job. But my heart wasn't in it. Then I thought I might go back to Chicago with the money I had, get a job and an apartment and live there. I had always liked the city. Things were more pleasant at home and I figured I could stay there until I found what I wanted.

Besides, it sounded like my mother needed help. She didn't say what was going on, but the hints she let slip didn't sound good, such as my grandmother getting old and unwell, the ongoing problems with Marty, the fact that she even mentioned she was having trouble coping.

My folks were delighted when I told them. My mother said, "We'd be happy to have you stay here until you get settled. Don't worry about a thing."

I made the arrangements and kept repeating to myself that I wasn't wimping out. I had been gone two years when I had been supposed to stay two weeks. I had learned a bunch about what I could do and what I couldn't. I had grown up, I was twenty-four and it was time to use the money and experience I had saved up. It would be different at home. I was different. My mother was different. I'd look for a job, hopefully in publishing, and maybe meet someone special. I was tired of being lonely.

The night before I left, my friends on the floor gave me a going-away party. Al said he would never get another tenant as nice as me. I was starting to choke up.

Lise kissed me and said she was happy that now I would find my true profession, whatever it was. I said she was being déclassé and walked away.

Howie hugged me and gave me a big smooch on the mouth. He said he felt like he was losing something he hadn't really found.

He said, "Stay. We'll make a go of it." He said it movie gangster style, rasping the words.

Then Roy handed me a book, an old edition of "The Count of Monte Cristo," bound in peeling leather, with a signature in French I couldn't read.

"Remember me when you read this," he said. He pressed my hand and looked like he was going to cry, then he hugged me, holding me close. I hugged him back and felt like crying too. I didn't want to let go, feeling suddenly I couldn't stand it if I never saw him again. My insides churned in a peculiar way. We broke apart and stared at each other.

I said, "Thank you," clutching the book.

It seemed I was losing something I had been searching for, and hadn't known I'd found -- until I'd lost it.

AUTHOR'S NOTE

It must have been the pictures on my wall that kept me from changing the names of my parents and relatives in this memoir. I began with everyone anonymous but then found I couldn't write about my family. The pictures, when I looked at them for inspiration, or to jog my memory, answered only to the names they had always had, who they really were.

When I wrote about everyone else, the anonymity sparked my memory of things that had happened and I was able to write about them more completely than if I had used their real names.